White Boy from the Townships
*From Apartheid to Freedom, the memoir of a white American
DJ immersed in black South African Culture*

James Eoppolo

DEDICATION

To my loving wife, Charlottie who made all things possible.

Introduction

This is as close as I can come to fully explaining my personal history with the people, culture, politics and history of South Africa. This is a somewhat complete accounting of a white American radio broadcaster who created, wrote, produced and presented a program which highlighted culture's role in the anti-apartheid struggle within South Africa. The program was called *Amandla! Music of South Africa*. From conception to the end, the program had a total lifespan of more than 12 years, airing in Philadelphia from February 1990 through April 1998. During this time I had the pleasure of interviewing, and coming to know many of South Africa's foremost recording artists and prominent political figures. Excerpts from several of these interviews appear throughout these pages. The impact from the program, as well as the impact from related experiences, was felt long after the final broadcast.

When I first conceived the idea for the program I fully intended to keep a journal of my experiences, whatever they happened to be. That was back in 1986, and except for a few sparse pages, I never committed another word to paper. Perhaps, I imagined a day when I would actually take the time to write it all down; or at least the majority of it anyway. If you are a South African, there will be references to people, places, and events that you may feel need no explanation. If you happen to be non-South African, you may feel that these references require additional explanation. Sorry one and all. It took me this long to finally sit down and do this, and I did not see the need to make this an extensively detailed South African history book, there are thousands of those you can research and enjoy.

While I am proud to have played a tiny role in the recent history of South Africa, I am *not* an historian. It is my hope, if something contained in these pages captures your imagination, please take some time, do a little research, and enrich your understanding. That was the primary reason for my creating the program in the first place. When *Amandla!* ended in mid-1998, I foolishly believed that my emotional connection to South Africa ended with it. I have always felt that my experience was so personal I would never be able to adequately capture it with words on a page. Yet, here I sit, writing down thoughts and memories that stretch back decades.

Awakening

It is twenty-five minutes past ten in the morning, and my eyes can hardly focus. Somehow, my body has managed to bend itself into a position of moderate comfort. After a grueling two hours, the findings are in; the plastic chairs in the temporary international terminal at the Brussels Airport were not designed for comfort, and certainly not for sleep. I have no idea how large of a country Belgium may be, but judging by this terminal, a postage stamp serves as my analogy. With another 7 hours to fill, and no likelihood of sleep, now seems the perfect time to attempt to answer a question I have been asked more times than I can count, "how did you get involved with South Africa?" Good question, pull up a chair.

I suppose the *how* is directly linked to family, religion, and murder. Pretty much in that order. I was born on a steamy summer day in July 1954, the second son of three to the son of an Italian immigrant and the daughter of a dirt-poor sharecropper from Mississippi. As I was to learn later, it was the same year that the United States Supreme Court struck down the practice of segregation in public schools across the country. A great victory in the civil rights movement, although it would be many years before it was enacted in every state. Meanwhile, in South Africa that year, civil rights took a beating, literally, as the new Natives Resettlement Act allowed for forced removal of blacks from areas around Johannesburg. Strange, even in the year of my birth, race was playing a role in my development. The city of my birth was Wilmington, Delaware; ever hear of it?

I'm not surprised, most people say, "No." Situated on the Mid-Atlantic coast of the United States, Wilmington sits about 33 miles south of Philadelphia, Pennsylvania. Home to millions, Philly, as it's lovingly called, is often referred to as *the birthplace of democracy* thanks to the fact that this historic city is where the Declaration of Independence and the United States Constitution were drafted and signed. As a mid-sized city, Wilmington is rather a non-descript place. There's nothing terribly great about it, nor is there anything horribly wrong with it. You're close to all the major cultural and sports attraction in Philly without having to live in a densely populated area. Wilmington once had a slogan emblazoned on all of the signs greeting visitors entering the city; it read *Welcome to Wilmington, A Place to be Somebody*. A little more than 100,000 people were trying to *be somebody* in the mid-1950s and 60s, mostly lower and middle class whites.

The more upwardly mobile were heading to the suburbs sprouting up north of the city. Some would say *fleeing* is a more accurate description. Most of the white population lived in the Western and Northern sections of the city, while the roughly17,000 black citizens lived either in poverty or in lower and middle class status on the east side of town. My family fell under the lower middle class category, living in a rented house on the West side among other white families much like our own. If I saw a black person it was the random pedestrian passing through our neighborhood on their way back to the east side, or to what many whites routinely called *Niggerville*. In other cities across the county *Niggertown* was the accepted moniker. No, I'm not making this up.

My father was a city fire fighter; earning a salary that barely kept a roof over our heads and food on the table. As a result, he was forced to work a variety of side jobs on his days off. Days off. I don't think the man knew what those were until he retired. Laying carpet, delivering carpet, delivering appliances, landscaping, the list is endless. I could never figure out where he got his sense of duty to his family, or his energy to keep going for that matter. At the age of 5 he lost his mother to tuberculosis on Christmas morning; Merry Christmas indeed. His father died not long after. Alcohol was his killer. Older siblings were dumped into orphanages and foster homes; while my father along with a younger sister, were raised by relatives. To this day I have never asked him where he learned this sense of duty, but I don't have to think very hard to know where I learned mine.

My mother was of course a stay at home mom. It's what most women did in those days. The last born into a family of 13, she was raised in the delta region of 1930s Mississippi. Her family followed the cotton crop from plantation to plantation all across the state. At the age of 13 she lost her father to a heart attack and older brothers brought her north to Delaware. My mother has always found it difficult to share memories about her life in Mississippi she'd say, "Shit, there's nothing memorable about going hungry and living in a shack." She did chose to remember how on some days after school she and her sister Nellie were instructed to go across the field to the shack of Aunt Sara.

A black woman of commanding presence, Aunt Sara would watch the children while parents, black and white were busy in the cotton fields. She was also authorized to deliver a good scolding if needed. While the family knew nothing of material wealth, they did have music. Her father and all of her brothers loved to play music.

Guitars, fiddles, mandolins were the instruments of choice. After a hot day in the fields picking cotton, summer evenings were filled with homemade music drifting in to their shack from the small front porch. Once, after I had nagged her about it, she told me that on many an evening a few of the black and equally poor sharecroppers would cross through the fields, guitars in hand, to sit out on the porch and swap songs and tunes with her father and brothers. The whites teaching fiddle tunes and country hits of the day; the blacks teaching the unique style of bottleneck blues guitar. Poverty and music, it does bring people together. While my mother did not play an instrument, she did play the radio, constantly. My earliest memories include hearing my mother sing along with the sounds of country, rock and roll, and soul music on the little portable radio in the kitchen. Music, it seemed, had the power to brighten her day.

When I was old enough to care for it, I was given a small transistor radio which quickly became a constant companion. Its tiny, static filled speaker fed my hungry ears with the sounds of the Beatles, Temptations, Rolling Stones, Supremes and more. The images painted by my mother and the exposure to a wide variety of music had a profound impact on the direction that my life would take. Working in radio as a disc jockey was the future I always pictured for myself. What a cool job, present new music and kindle memories with the old. From ages 6 to 13, I attended Saint Anthony of Padua, a private, all white, very Catholic grade school. Education, discipline and religious studies; were all administered, with great bravado I might add, by Franciscan nuns. Did I mention discipline?

Dressed in long black robes, and headgear called a *habit,* leaving only their round faces showing, these ladies were not permitted to marry. They had willingly given themselves to God to work in his service. Many of us felt that they took this path for no other reason than the legal right to beat the hell out of children; which they did to me quite often. Beatings with heavy rulers, being locked in a closet, slaps and even punches to the face were all part of their repertoire. It was their way of keeping 100 students per class under control. As we grew, we used to think the violence was a result of pent up sexual tension waxing and waning, who knows?

In these environments of neighborhood and of school, my personal exposure to people of color was virtually non-existent. Don't get me wrong, at school we regularly saw pictures of the pa*gan babies* whose souls our pennies and nickels helped to save. The pictures were always the same; smiling African children in loincloth looking thankful because our money helped to bring salvation through Jesus. For all I knew, I may have been seeing my first South Africans.

It's no surprise that my thoughts about people other than white were more than a little tainted. Schoolmates and neighborhood friends used the N word with regularity, telling fear-inducing tales of violent, anti-white ways. "Niggers", I was told, "are dangerous and can't be trusted." Television news and newspapers in the early and mid-1960s carried frightening stories that seemed to verify these facts. Black people always looked angry on TV.

They were always marching in cities across America, carrying signs, shouting, singing, and fighting with police. What did the *Civil Rights Movement* mean anyway? Fold these in with news of the divisive Vietnam War, and you can see; this was scary stuff to a child. My parents would throw the N word around from time to time. It was usually part of a frustrating venting during tougher than normally tough economic times, times when furniture was repossessed, car repairs took the battered checkbook in to the red, or a child, namely me, needed new and very expensive eye glasses to replace the pair I had broken.

For my mother the use of the *N* word was something she learned in Delaware, and not surprisingly from her youth in Mississippi, a notoriously racist state. *Colored* was the word she was taught to use in those days. Lower and middle class whites often directed their frustrations at black people because they "were all on welfare while I'm working my ass off!" On more occasions than I can remember I heard my father sigh while sitting at the kitchen table checkbook in hand and exclaim, "No matter what we do, we never get ahead." It was his mantra. Despite my learned suspicion and fear of black people, a puzzling question began to trouble my young mind. It started to take definitive shape somewhere around my 11th birthday. "How could my devout Catholic schoolmates pray to Jesus Christ one minute, and then condemn an entire race of people the next?"

I was more than a little confused and the answers were extremely cloudy until the evening of April 4th, 1968. When James Earl Ray pulled the trigger and Dr. Martin Luther King Jr. fell dead, I was reborn at the age of 13. That night, I heard schoolmates at our Catholic Youth Group celebrate because "they killed the nigger." As I write this passage, I can still hear their adolescent voices and feel the same sickness that turned my stomach more than 40 years ago. Thankfully, I also feel the same sense of salvation that swept over me that night. It is a feeling I best describe as my awakening. Like a thunderbolt from God; or an angel's hand touching mine. Feel free to imagine the metaphor or analogy of your own choosing. It may be impossible to explain what I felt that night; but I pray that you recognize those moments in your own life.

In the days and weeks that followed Dr. King's murder, inner cities across the country, including Wilmington, erupted with rioting. Looting, fire bombings and reports of sniper fire directed at emergency personnel, like my fire fighter father, resulted in then Governor Terry activating the National Guard to Wilmington to "restore order and keep the peace." There were several mornings that would find my father arriving home from having worked overnight to report that he and his comrades were showered with rocks and bottles as they attempted to fight blazes set by rioting youth. Meanwhile, local television news programs and newspapers were filled with images of troops armed with M-1 rifles and machine gun equipped Army Jeeps patrolling the streets, "protecting businesses and citizens" officials would proclaim. At the outset of this deployment no one could have predicted that the overly paranoid Governor Terry would order the troops to remain on the streets until January 1969, nine full months; despite the mayor pleading to pull the troops out. Thanks to Governor Terry, Wilmington has the distinct honor of being the site of the longest military occupation of any city in America since the Civil War. To South Africans, whether living in townships or in posh suburbs, all of this probably sounds like a walk in the park. That August, while black anger had cooled to just below the boiling point, another event witnessed on television fortified the new way in which I viewed the world.

The 1968 Democratic National Convention in Chicago, Illinois. Since President Lyndon Johnson had announced that he would not be seeking re-election, the purpose of the convention was a simple one; nominate Vice President Hubert Humphrey as the Democratic Nominee for the Presidency. What could go wrong?

In the months leading up to Chicago, the nation was in turmoil from the assassination of Dr. King and the riots that followed. The convention also came on the heels of the assassination of presidential front-runner Senator Robert Kennedy, gunned down in June. Countless anti-war protests against the U.S. involvement and mounting death toll in Vietnam added fuel to the fire, a fire that 10,000 protesters planned to bring to Chicago during the convention. No surprise then that Mayor Richard Daley made it very clear that "his city" would be a showcase of law and order. 23,000 police and National Guard troops were going to ensure he'd have his way. How strange is it that in the same year we see a virtual police state established in the cities across America, and thousands of miles away, the formation of the South African Bureau of State Security, BOSS for short takes place.

So there I was, disillusioned thanks to the load of bullshit I had been fed about black people, and now feeling that the Vietnam War was insane! I watched the convention with intense interest. Could Humphrey really bring about change? Are things going to get better in this country? The answer was revealed sooner than later.

On the afternoon of August 28th, the third day of the convention, the Chicago police apparently had had enough of even peaceful demonstrations. They rushed into the crowd savagely beating protesters, who in turn pelted them with rocks, food and pieces of concrete. Later that night, as police violence erupted once again, protesters chanted, "the whole world is watching." A now 14-year old boy was watching, and it steered his thinking even further to the left.

The fall of '68 saw a Presidential election that put Richard M. Nixon in the White House. Fear was a big factor in his victory, and his subsequent re-election four years later; fear of black and white radicals overthrowing the government, and fear of the yellow devils in Vietnam. I like to think that the majority of voting Americans suffered from some form of temporary insanity. Thankfully, the Watergate scandal of illegally spying on opponents would eventually bring him down. With the Vietnam War raging, racial tensions dancing on a razor's edge, and *Planet of the Apes* in movie theaters, *somehow appropriate for the times,* young James had another epiphany.

At my choosing, I began my high school years at Wilmington High, a public school where the student population was more than seventy-five percent black, even the Principal, Dr. Jimmie V. Morris was black! To many of my former friends this seemed to be an insane choice. I heard "Go to school with niggers? Are you crazy?" Record numbers of white students chose to flee the city for the safety of suburban schools. For me the diversity was exhilarating. In no time my best friends were Bob Simmons and Bill Macklin, both the color of the people I was warned to avoid! Bob always wore a broad smile and walked with a visible bounce in his step. He moved seamlessly between the two worlds of white and black. From angry, politicized black students, to the *hippie-radical* type white students, one of which I was quickly becoming, Bob could hang with them all. Bill on the other hand was more drawn to Jimi Hendrix and Bob Dylan than to Marvin Gaye or The Temptations. He played acoustic guitar, was a passionate poet and as a result was somewhat ostracized by some of the tougher brothers.

It was here, with help from Bob and Bill that I was politicized. Many of my new found friends were members of local organizations affiliated with the Black Panther Party. Founded in Oakland, California in 1966, The Panthers were a revolutionary party with chapters across the country. Dressed in black leather jackets, sporting black berets and often seen carrying shotguns and hand guns, these brothers and sisters scared the shit out of white people. Their calls for *Black Power,* and the attitude that *white people can't fix it for us, we have to do it ourselves* is frequently credited with being the inspiration for the Black Conciseness movement within South Africa years later.

The Black Panther Party had become an attractive alternative for young people who felt that the days of non-violent protest died with Dr. King. It was time for action, violent action if need be. Lively discussions about revolution, race relations, the riots in cities across America and the kind of future we imagined for our children filled my time inside and outside of class. Friends turned me on to hip black authors past and present and I soaked it up like a sponge. We forged a mutual trust and respect for each other.

This was evident when on the first anniversary of Dr. King's murder I was stopped in the hall between classes and tipped off by a friend, "make sure you're not in the halls this afternoon at 2. We're all walking out in honor of Dr. King. There might be some nasty shit going down." I didn't ask what sort of nasty shit but since my class at 2 was located on the second floor and looked out over the front entrance of the school, I knew I'd have a ringside seat. At precisely 2:00 all of the black students in my social studies class rose from their desks and calmly walked out of the room. The teacher, who had no idea what prompted this mass exit, did nothing more than stare, with a look of total confusion plastered on her face. Within minutes hundreds of black students had assembled on the sidewalk and front steps of the school. The few of us who were left inside the classroom raced to the windows to watch the drama unfold below us

As this sea of young black faces chanted with fists in the air our attention was drawn to the main road where a convoy of state police cruisers, sirens and lights equally ablaze, appeared out of nowhere. They quickly blocked off the road and exited their vehicles armed with shotguns. As best they could, the police tried to encircle the crowd, but made no moves to disperse them. Was this the nasty shit my friend had mentioned? Sure seemed like it. The chanting kept up and grew louder, along with the tension. After 10 minutes or so, Principal Morris came out to speak to the police and then to the students.

Despite the fact that he had broken new ground that year by becoming the first black principal, Dr. Morris, a very mild mannered gentleman, was called "Uncle Tom" by many of the radical black students. We all knew this was a volatile situation. We couldn't hear what was being said, but the exchange was clearly heated and went on for some time. Then as quickly as they had appeared the state police, shotguns now lowered, got back in to their cars and departed. Slowly the crowd began to break up, most came back inside, some set off for home. We learned later that the promise of a student assembly to honor Dr. King is what brought this extraordinary confrontation to a peaceful end. For reasons unknown, Dr. Jimmie V. Morris would serve only two years as principal before being replaced by an upbeat, white, 30-something southerner named Mr. McGann.

Meanwhile, my street and political education continued as I caulked up average grades. I had no interest in going to college; working on the radio was my destiny, so why bother? I'd study what I liked, hung out with friends and watched as black and Latino and black and white students would fight it out, sometimes with knives, mostly with fists. I confess to being more than a little bit amused when a few of my former, racist white friends from catholic school got their asses kicked in a fight. In our junior year, Bob and I, forever the radicals drafted a Declaration of Student Rights. Among other things, we demanded an equal say in choosing guest speakers, when and where we could organize rallies and the right to distribute publications from the Black Panthers and radical white groups. We presented our Declaration to Mr. McGann who read it, placed it back on his desk, smiled and said "There is no way in hell you're getting this approved. You can go now." So much for student rights.

Imagine our surprise when in our senior year Bob and I heard our names announced over the school's PA system summoning us to the Principal's office. When we arrived his secretary politely ushered us in to see him. He flashed the same smile from last year and we figured this was probably the smile of expulsion. From the corner of his desk he picked up a piece of paper and held it up to show it to us. Was this our official "You're Expelled" paperwork? No. To our disbelief, it was our Declaration of Student Rights! "Remember this from last year?" he asked. "Well, we would like the two of you to help us implement it this year."

Again, he hit us with that frigging smile. Bob and I were allies; when it came to authority and such, we shared a common brain. Before I could say it, Bob smiled back and in the kindest of voices said, "Thank you, but you threw us out of your office last year when we presented it." I knew where he was going with this so I picked up the conversation. "And since we're graduating, we don't really care what happens this year or after we leave." That ended the meeting, and there was no smile as we left. We did hear a year or so later that the Declaration was in fact instituted. Victory was ours even if we're weren't there to savor it.

Perhaps the most influential aspect of my senior year was Black History studies. Wilmington High School became the first school in the state to offer it as an elective course. To my amazement, I was the only white student to take the class. For the life of me, I couldn't figure out why white people DIDN'T want to learn about black people. After having lived a completely white childhood, I had an insatiable appetite to learn all that I could. Mr. Stanley Williams, a young black teacher, lover of literature and music, a jazz drummer himself, was my Guru. He was asked by the state if he'd like to develop this course, and instructed to do whatever he wanted. What he did was change lives, mine included. W.E.B. Dubois, Eldridge Cleaver, Marcus Garvey, Fredrick Douglas, we read them, discussed them, talked of slavery, debated race and much more.

Oddly enough, South Africa and apartheid was never mentioned. Most black Americans had their own problems I guess. On numerous occasions the all-white suburban schools would transfer an innocent, or shall we say *racially ignorant* student to our school for the day. It was a way for them to learn about black people in the bush, otherwise known as the inner-city.

One day a pretty blonde sat in on our Black History class. Mr. Williams could see that she was nervous beyond words, so he introduced her and asked if she wouldn't mind sharing her impressions of the day. With great hesitation she stood up in the front and between nervous gulps of air said, "Before I came here today I thought every black person carried a knife or a baseball bat ready to kill me. Now, I can see that you're just like me." One student sitting near me couldn't resist himself and in voice filled with false anger said "I'll show you a knife!" She recoiled and turned a shade whiter. Mr. Williams admonished the joker and assured the pretty blonde that she was safe. The remainder of the class was spent talking openly about prejudice based on preconceived ideas and the need for dialogue such as this. It took me 40 years to do it, but I recently tracked down Mr. Williams and expressed my undying gratitude for his vital role in helping to shape the man I would become. During those 4 years I discovered my humanity, or what the Zulu people call *Ubuntu*. It was also when I met Charlottie, the woman who would become my dearest friend, wife and inspiration.

From a Seed

Just one short year after graduating from high school, I married the love of my life, Charlottie. She was and remains the most kind, and compassionate woman I have ever known. Her capacity to put a positive spin on the worst of situations has saved me an endless number of times. Despite our youthful age of 19, both of us felt that spending our lives together should begin sooner than later; a decision neither has yet to regret. The daughter of a Native-American - Mexican mother and German father, Charlottie is endowed with the combination of an inherent respect for the earth and all creatures upon it, and an orderly, analytical mind that masters whatever challenge she faces. None of what I have done, or will ever do in my adult life would be possible without her. As planned, my career in broadcasting began on the heels of my marriage, and in 1976 we found ourselves living in the northeastern state of New Hampshire, with me working at a local radio station.

It was the flag-waving year of the U.S. Bi-centennial, and the country was going commercially wild celebrating 200 years of democracy. My first true awakening to apartheid manifested itself in thinly detailed newswire stories concerning some sort of civil unrest. The apartheid government did what it could to keep their escalating violence against the youth of South Africa off of front pages around the world.

All I knew boiled down to isolated stories about rioting students and police brutality, nothing that exposed the real situation on the ground. I confess that outside of hearing the name *Mandela* a few times, South Africa and the plight of its oppressed people slipped from my mind for several years, besides we had another Presidential election in the works. That all changed when my more hands-on involvement with the culture, people and politics of South Africa began in earnest during the early 1980s.

While working at a radio station in my hometown of Wilmington, Delaware, an unusual LP record album arrived. It was indicated on the sleeve that this was South African in origin, and while I was familiar with a few artists from Africa such as the Afro-fusion band Osibisa, and some of the jazz influenced Highlife music of Ghana; this LP contained music like none I had heard before. An acoustic guitar fired off an opening flourish in an exciting tuning that made me wonder where this was headed. Then, a deep bass guitar kicked in and thumped out a beat very much in the foreground of the mix. An accordion provided additional melody. The rhythms moved in patterns unique to my ears. People have often asked me to describe what I felt or what captured my attention when I first heard this music. I am unable to answer them.

For me, music is organic; it lives and breathes, and has immense power. Even being a musician myself, I cannot put into words why some music sends chills up the back of my neck, or makes me cry or dance. These new sounds from South Africa did all of that, and I'll be damned if I can remember the artist! I would later learn that this music was called *Maskanda* or Zulu guitar music. A few months later, as South African State President P.W. Botha and Foreign Minister Pik Botha crisscrossed Europe trying to convince everyone that apartheid wasn't really so bad; two other South Africans impacted my life in ways never imagined.

Their band was called Juluka, *sweat* in the language of the Zulu people; and in 1984, Johnny Clegg and his Zulu partner Sipho Mchunu burst upon the American music scene via MTV. The video was *Scatterlings of Africa*. Besides the obvious multi-racial make-up of Juluka, there were numerous aspects of this band and their music that kept me riveted to the television. They sang in English and Zulu, making their music: their message if you will, that much more accessible across cultural boundaries. They had taken the *Maskanda* style and made it very contemporary; electric guitars, deep drum and bass backing, with equally deep male backing vocals. Johnny, Sipho and the band carried a respect for the traditional, but also shouted out *this is new music!* If that wasn't enough, visually Juluka was every bit as exciting as their music! The video featured high kicking Zulu dance steps, scenes of stick fighting, the band adorned with traditional beadwork; all interwoven with footage shot in townships and rural villages.

America had never seen a band like this before. It was another one of those magical music moments when the chill raced up the back of my neck. I was hooked and had to find additional South African music to satisfy my new interest. That, I discovered, proved to be the proverbial needle in a haystack. Sure, you could find jazz great Hugh Masekela and Miriam Makeba records; they'd been in the U.S. for decades having fled South Africa, but their varying styles didn't satisfy my craving. Many a record store employee shot me a puzzled look when I would ask for *other* South African music. I did manage to obtain promotional information about Juluka from their U.S. record label. At least that provided some insight into the style and history of Johnny and Sipho. How as a teen, Johnny became fascinated with Zulu culture, frequenting the workers' hostels around Johannesburg; there he learned the basics of *Maskanda* guitar.

How he and Sipho met as young men and played as an acoustic duo around the city; despite the tough apartheid laws restricting such public displays of unity. How they persevered to become stars in South Africa. Clegg spoke of how metaphor was an important tool in telling the South African story. It was both traditional and often necessary because of government censoring of lyrics that spoke out against apartheid. I had to learn more. More about other artists and styles of music never heard outside of the country, more about apartheid, and the people of South Africa. It was off to the library to begin learning, absorbing.

Except for *Juluka,* the search for music kept coming up empty, my search for knowledge about culture, apartheid, Mandela and the worldwide movement to bring about change was bountiful. I read of the dehumanizing brutality of apartheid, rekindling images of racial hatred and violence of the American south. I learned about economic, cultural, sport and even academic boycotts; of the *Free Mandela* rallies that had taken place in London, Washington D.C. and other cities around the world. I felt ashamed that my former radicalism had somehow let all of this slip past me. Where the hell had I been? *"I ain't gonna play Sun City"* One by one a wide range of music superstars sang the lyrics with swagger and pride.

This was the most high-profile cultural assault against apartheid to date. It came in October of 1985 arriving, like *Juluka,* in the form of a music video. Written by guitarist Steven Van Zandt, a member of Bruce Springsteen's renowned *E Street Band,* the song railed against artists who had performed at the lavish Sun City Casino in South Africa, despite a United Nations cultural boycott. While it was never a commercial success, it got a substantial amount of press. It would also provide a large dose of fuel to the raging fire around the cultural boycott the following year.

Fast forward to August 1986, and the word on the lips of disc jockeys and music fans around the world was *Graceland*, Paul Simon's ground breaking recording that would help steer me onto a path where I would meet some of South Africa's greatest musicians, anti-apartheid leaders, and to establish deep friendships that continue to this day. Music critics armed with more descriptive verbiage than I ever care to read, or to use, have dissected this recording every way possible. Forgive me if I just say it was a unique blending of pure South African rhythms, coupled with Simons' poetic lyrics. Having sold in excess of eight million copies, suffice it to say, the recording was, and still is popular.

If you are not familiar with the recording, you probably should stop reading now.

As *Graceland* picked up speed on the record charts, a few record labels, never slow to exploit an opportunity, released a small number of compilation CDs featuring South African music. Some of the new releases included roughly translated lyrics. A man kisses his wife at the rural train station as he heads off for *eGoli* (*place of gold-Johannesburg*) to work in the mines. A poor woman cries out for coal which she can't afford, and it's freezing outside. Children are told not to cry, their father will return from prison one day.

On the surface simple stories, until you place them in the context of apartheid South Africa. When you do, you understand the plight of mine workers who travel hundreds of miles from their families to work the mines and live in horrendous blocks of hostels. Of the staggering poverty in townships throughout the country, and of children longing for their fathers jailed under oppressive apartheid laws. These compilation CDs were a nice spin-off, but more importantly, I became convinced that culture, especially music and song, played a vital role in the mass democratic movement within South Africa. Despite its staggering mass appeal, *Graceland* was just the tip of the iceberg…there was more to this music than a danceable beat. It had power, power to change the course of history.

It's funny how the growing success of *Graceland* suddenly put South Africa in the news a bit more. From the fall of '86 and on into 1987, there was an uptick in stories about the State of Emergency; magazines and newspapers ran articles detailing the creation and violent implementation of apartheid. The United States government really ratcheted up the pressure by instituting sanctions. South African Airways was forbidden to land on U.S. soil. Bans against buying South African minerals, agricultural products, textiles, and coal, were also put in place. If they hadn't done so already, corporations were under pressure to divest any and all interest in South Africa.

Calls for the unbanning of the African National Congress and its imprisoned leaders, including the *hero* of the movement, Nelson Mandela grew louder. Anti-apartheid rallies became more wide spread and noticed in the states and around the world. Music helped people sit up and take notice of oppression; how cool was that? Perhaps it was always so and I just failed to pay attention, like so many other people around me. No longer. I was reading whatever I could get my hands on to understand the history past and present.

When *Graceland* exploded, I was working at one of the highest rated music stations in Philadelphia, and felt on top of my game. Of course we were playing the hell out of the *Graceland* project and that's when my thoughts turned to using the medium I knew so well to tell an audience, any audience, how culture was helping to keep the people strong in heart and mind. As I envisioned it, the program would feature an extensive variety of musical styles from South Africa, old and new. The relevance of the music would be explained in an effort to teach American listeners about its vital role. Critical to the program, *live* updates from the townships or Johannesburg, My hope was to find a professional DJ or Presenter who, in addition to talking about music, was willing to provide first hand accounts of what was happening on the ground. No sterile news, these reports should convey the emotions connected to the turbulent times. Of course the host should be South African. Where to start? Honestly, I had no idea whatsoever.

As fate would have it, sorry for the cliché but it was indeed fateful that the Chief Engineer at the radio station walked into my studio, dropped a magazine on my desk saying, "There's something in there about a South African guy and I know you're into that." The magazine was *Broadcast Engineering*, interesting only if you happen to be a Broadcast Engineer. Inside was an article highlighting Johnny Clegg's producer Hilton Rosenthal who had left South Africa and was now living in Los Angeles. He had launched his own record label, *Rhythm Safari,* and the article detailed recording techniques, studio equipment, and of course, the popularity of *Graceland.*

Hilton was responsible for supplying a curious Paul Simon with a stack of South African recordings months before Simon traveled to the country. "Hmmm," I said to no one in particular. "I'm in broadcasting, I love his production style, he is a South African in the music business, why not call him and run my idea by him?" Shortly after a call to directory information for L.A., I was on the phone with Hilton. I introduced myself, told him that I was a longtime fan of Juluka and of his production style. Hilton has a way of making drums deeper than deep; they penetrate inside of you, touching your soul. I then went on to explain my idea. Hilton was immediately sold and quickly and kindly began to rattle off the names, phone and fax numbers of numerous South African record labels and their management along with a contact at Radio 702, perhaps the most popular station in all of South Africa.

Hilton understood that a white American having anything to do with *explaining* black South African music and the political climate would be problematic at best. He suggested that I speak with Johnny for guidance. As a white South African deeply immersed in Zulu culture, Johnny knew firsthand the intense scrutiny likely to come my way. A few weeks later, Clegg and his new band *Savuka (we have awakened)* were in the states promoting a new CD, and a new sound. It was called *Third World Child.* Johnny's partner in *Juluka,* Sipho Mchunu had decided that he was finished with a musician's life on the road; he left the band and returned to his beloved home in the region of KwaZulu Natal, in the eastern part of the country. One afternoon while Clegg was in Los Angeles, I phoned him from Philadelphia.

Hilton had briefed him on my reason for wanting to talk, and Johnny was very receptive. We also talked about this new musical direction with *Savuka.* His lyrics had become noticeably more open and radical. Take for instance the track *Asimbonanga (Mandela)*-meaning *We have not seen Mandela.* The song describes the imprisonment of Mandela and of people longing for his release. It also includes the solemn naming of fallen heroes, several of whom were killed by the apartheid regime. The track was banned from the airwaves by the government controlled South African Broadcasting Corporation *(SABC).*

Johnny explained, "In the past few years, this country has been on the verge of a civil war. With the State of Emergency, more and more people are being killed and detained every day." In a grave voice that held nothing back he continued. "This government is using third force elements to fan the flames and create violence in the townships and rural areas. I decided, I can no longer just write love songs, or use metaphor to express what I feel." The title track *Third World Child*, also banned by the SABC, put it bluntly. *The future calls his name out loud, echoed on the violence of the guns.*

After explaining the concept of this yet un-named radio program in detail, Johnny offered his support to do what he could, followed by a word of advice that I took to heart. "James, if you do this, you must make yourself so knowledgeable on all things South African no-one could ever question your credibility." With Johnny's words of caution etched in my mind, it was time to fit another piece to the puzzle. This would require a well-crafted letter and a train ride to New York City. The *caution* part was a no-brainer. Despite all the excitement and praise generated by the *Graceland* recording and subsequent tour, Paul Simon was stung by serious verbal and media attacks for breaking the cultural boycott against apartheid South Africa. He had gone to Johannesburg in 1984 to record basic tracks for a possible future project; a trip frowned upon by many in the anti-apartheid community.

He was also accused of being a *cultural bandit,* someone whose only interest was using South African rhythms and styles to rejuvenate his own career, which at the time was thought to be failing. Frequently he explained that he went there for musical, not political purposes. Even with many South African musicians coming to his defense, he continued to come under fire. Now, decades later, mention the *Graceland* project to South Africans, and a lively debate will ensue.

"A policy of racial segregation is necessarily based on doctrines of racial discrimination" This was the first United Nations declaration on apartheid, it was issued a little more than two years after the implementation of apartheid as law by the National Party in 1948. The declaration had virtually no impact whatsoever. Harsh words mean nothing to an oppressive government. More than a decade would pass before the UN Special Committee against Apartheid would convene for the first time. Its purpose was to provide more bite to the anti-apartheid movement by pressing for increased and stricter sanctions and boycotts, assisting victims of apartheid, and raising international awareness. It was this committee that operated as the cultural watchdog as well, taking note, and making public the names of entertainment, literary and even academic celebrities that performed or appeared in South Africa.

Before I took another step forward, I wanted to make damn certain that my idea for the radio program would not violate the terms of the cultural boycott. I posted a letter to the office of the chairman of the committee and laid out my idea in great detail, along with my background in the media. The letter included a request to meet, which I had hoped would allow me the opportunity to pitch it in person. Off it went, and the waiting began. To my surprise, a letter from the committee arrived a few weeks later. It advised me that my letter had been passed on to the New York City offices of the exiled African National Congress. The name mentioned had a familiar ring to it, Barbara Masekela, the sister of jazz great Hugh Masekela.

Barbara was the head of the ANC's Department of Arts and Culture and a steadfast believer in the power of culture to bring about change. It made perfect sense that my letter would be forwarded to her. Alone in my studio I nervously made the call to her office. From the start, she was receptive and quick to suggest a meeting. She invited me to meet with several ANC Department of Arts and Culture members who also worked closely with the U.N. committee. In a matter of weeks I was on a train bound for New York City to meet with members of an organization declared to be *terrorists* by my own government. Would they *look* like terrorists? Were they going to hate this white man the minute they saw me? I made a point of not bringing anything written down. I wanted them to see and hear my passion and dedication for this undertaking.

Arriving at the office I was met at the door by a twenty-something black man in a tailored suit and tie. For the life of me I will never be able to remember his name or the names of the two other ANC members who joined us in a relaxed exchange sitting around a table. Terrorists? They were full of smiles and laughs, and were quite enthusiastic, if not a little bit amused, at the thought of this white American taking such an interest. My idea of exploring and exposing culture's role in the movement was given their full support. Before we parted, they urged me to contact the ANC representative in Philadelphia, a Mr. Godfrey Sithole. They assured me that he would be a most valuable comrade. That would prove to be a vast understatement.

Born in the KwaZulu/Natal province, Godfrey fled South Africa in 1962 along with 27 other ANC students, including future South African President Thabo Mbeki. As with so many South Africans, Godfrey's journey into exile delivered him to the United States. As I would learn, he and his wife Sibongile were part of an extensive South African community in and around Philadelphia supporting one another while raising awareness of the anti-apartheid movement. They would come to be my tutors in isiZulu, the language of the Zulu people, as well as invaluable contributors and friends. Having gained the approval of both the ANC and the UN Special Committee, what now? Find a host in South Africa!

Radio 702 has been hailed as the most successful radio stations in South African broadcasting history. It first hit the AM airwaves in 1980 before jumping over to the FM band in the mid-80s as a pop music station. Unique to broadcasting in the land of apartheid was their multi-racial air-staff; they had one black DJ, or Presenters by the name of Cocky "Two Bull" Tlhotlhalemaje. One black DJ. The walls of apartheid hadn't yet tumbled to the ground, still it was a start. Others were to follow, but I'm getting ahead of myself. Heard throughout the country by millions, Radio 702 was an unequaled powerhouse; and my wife and I found ourselves sitting across from its Managing Director Stan Katz. One of the primary contacts given to me by Johnny Clegg's producer Hilton Rosenthal, Katz was a legendary on-air host before moving on into management at 702. When I first contacted him via fax, *oh how spoiled we are today with texting, email and Skype*, he sent back a reply indicating that he would be in Washington D.C. the following month and wanted to meet.

Another train ride, this time south to D.C. Accompanied by my wife, I was armed with an extensively detailed outline of how I thought the program should be produced. The same sort of pitch made to the ANC, but this time in writing. We met in the café at Stan's hotel. After a brief bit of "hello, nice to meet you" I handed him my outline and started explaining the idea in full. While I explained, Stan spent his time looking past me at the various women coming and going, hardly ever making eye contact with me or looking at the outline.

I pressed on, he gazed on. When I finished, Stan said something along the lines of "Yeah, great. I think I've got the idea. I have a few great DJs who could do this. I'll talk with them and send you demos." And that was that. Oh, he did give me a Radio 702 coverage map.

We left feeling that an entire day as well as the cost of two round trip tickets was pissed away. There would be no demos, I was convinced of it. While I waited for the demos that I knew would never come, I set about collecting as broad a range of South African music as possible.

The management at the record labels that Hilton suggested responded with tremendous support. Dozens of LPs and cassettes began to make their way to me; many included extensive artist bios, proving to be a big asset. I continued to read everything I could get my hands on regarding South Africa, and was also receiving the anti-government newspaper The Weekly Mail, a week late, but still a considerable resource. Study, listen, and learn. Johnny Clegg's advice was running like a constant tape loop in my head.

Limpet mines, hand grenades, cross-border raids, car bombs. Dead children, dead soldiers, dead policemen, dead freedom fighters. There seemed to be no end in sight as 1988 bleed on. Stiff sanctions, disinvestment, and boycotts continued to mount pressure. Stories would sprout up that Nelson Mandela *might* be released, but another violent headline or blustery, defiant speech from President Botha would cause those hopes to quickly evaporate. Mandela's 70th birthday was fast approaching and a massive tribute concert was planned for Wembley Stadium in London. Music superstars from around the world were signing up to perform and show their support for his release, not that the apartheid regime would pay them any mind. There it was again though, music bringing people together, helping to shine the spotlight on oppression. Just as I began to formulate a new idea in an attempt to bring the program to life, the almost forgotten demos arrived from Stan Katz; three sixty minute cassettes, each with a name written across the label. Mesh Mapetla, Shado Twala and Cocky "Two Bull". There was nothing else in the package. No note, no bios, nothing. All I knew was Stan Katz said, "*they're great.*" I had no doubt that all three were great, but certainly not on these demos. While they did feature a wide range of music, they offered nothing in the way of explaining its relevance, or bothering to put it in to context. They did, a generic DJ show, little else. Didn't they read the detailed outline I gave to Stan? Did Stan even share it with them? I sent Stan a "thank you" filled fax, put the three cassettes into a drawer, and then put my next plan of attack into motion.

Qinisela! It was a word I would hear in song and a word I would come to use time and time again to inspire myself and others. It is a Zulu word that means *persevere*. As I became more or less consumed with getting this program on the air, somewhere, *qinisela* became my go to word. For almost two years I had immersed myself in the history, news and musical culture of South Africa. The record labels were constant supporters with new and old music, even though the program had not yet seen the light of day. The idea of using a South African DJ was no longer an option, so I decided to steer the project in an alternate direction. I would host and produce the program myself. I was confident that my deeper understand of the political and cultural history of South Africa would protect my credibility; but what about translations? For that I was going to need a lot of help. It was also imperative that I find either a DJ or journalist in South Africa willing to file the kind of live reports I imagined.

Since so much of the music I was receiving was sung in Zulu, and it is the most widely spoken of the eleven official languages in South Africa, I felt it necessary to acquire at least a basic knowledge of the language. With no such thing as the internet and its magical powers to guide me, it was call after call to bookstores in Philadelphia, Boston, and Washington D.C.. Each call produced the same result. Zulu?

Someone suggested calling universities offering African Studies. No luck in Philly, but I was tipped off that Yale University had an African Languages department. After a quick call to obtain the address, I sent off a letter outlining my idea and a plea for whatever assistance they could offer. Within two weeks a package arrived from Yale containing a photocopy version of the definitive Zulu language study guide *Learn Zulu* by C.L. Sibusiso Nyembezi. Sadly, I no longer have the note that came with it, nor do I remember the person who wrote it. I do remember that they wished me luck with my studies and the program. Another important bit of information was included, where I could purchase a basic Zulu language study tape! That act of kindness has remained special to me.

At last, with tape and book to guide me I began. *Sawubona* (Hello-singular) *Sanibonani* (Hello-plural) *Yebo* (Yes) *Cha* (No). The letter *C* requires a weird tongue sound that took some work to master. There were other noises I would have to learn. The letter *Q* is actually a click of the tongue. The letter *X* is not quite a click, but similar to the sound you would make to urge a horse to move. At least that's what the guide book said. The tape was helpful, but let's face it, not many of the songs contained lyrics like "how much does it cost?" or "where is the bathroom?" If this crazy idea was going to evolve into what I had hoped, I was going to need to study harder, and find a great tutor. I found two, my Philly ANC contact Godfrey Sithole and his dear, kind, and very patient wife Sibongile.

Somewhere between practicing my clicks, reading, listening and more reading, I placed a call to one of South Africa's most popular DJs, his name is Tim Modise. An executive at one of the record labels thought that Tim could easily provide the kind of insight and updated reports I was hoping for. On the surface I had to agree. Since he was a radio professional himself, he would fully understand how a radio program works and would make an excellent *live* source as stories unfolded. I couldn't have been more wrong. When I explained the concept of the program, as well as my clear ANC sympathies, Tim said, "I'll talk about music, but I can't afford to speak out about politics, I have a family and career to worry about." How could I fault the man? It was clear; finding someone willing to risk career and possibly personal safety to speak the truth was not going to come easily. Johnny Clegg to the rescue.

The UDF Unites-Apartheid Divides! Perhaps the most important anti-apartheid group during the 1980s, The United Democratic Front was a non-racial coalition of churches, student groups, unions and civic groups. Three million members strong, the UDF organized numerous rent boycotts, student protests, and worker's stay-aways. Many, including members of the apartheid regime, felt that the UDF was basically the banned ANC in disguise. For me, the UDF was my deliverance. Once again I have Johnny to thank for providing a contact at the cultural desk of the UDF, he in turn told me of a journalist by the name of Sipho Jacobs Ka-Khumalo, the editor of Jive Music Magazine.

Sipho had a long history as a news journalist and sports writer, plus, as editor of Jive, he was a wealth of knowledge and contacts in the South African music business. My long distance phone bill continued to soar, but this call was worth every penny. After only one conversation with Sipho, and an explanation of the program and his vital role, he responded with an exuberant "Yes!" The program was to be called *Amandla! Music of South Africa*. The word *Amandla* both Zulu and Xhosa and means *power*. For me, it was most appropriate.

It was now mid-1988 and the pieces were in place, all that was needed was an outlet. I produced a one-hour demo to shop around. It included a variety of music, from jazz to *mbaqanga*, the township style that first captured Paul Simon's imagination. The demo also included a report from Sipho detailing the importance of *shebeens*, the not-so legal drinking establishments in the township throughout South Africa. Shebeens serve as gathering places to meet friends, talk sports, enjoy music and discuss politics. They are a vital element to township life. Since the primary focus of the program was the role of culture in the mass democratic movement...i.e. to bring down apartheid, I explained the relevance of the lyrics as they pertained to life under apartheid. I was still a struggling, novice of a Zulu speaker, and understood none of the other indigenous languages. Godfrey, Sibongile and other local South Africans assisted with translating.

I was so convinced that the demo would result in a serious offer I applied for a visa to South Africa. The plan was a two week visit to conduct interviews, and gather hours of audio for the program. This undertaking afforded me my first personal dealings with the paranoid members of the South African Consulate. Two full months passed without a word on my application. One afternoon I received a phone call that went something like this. "This is Eugene de Klerk (*or some such name*) from the South African Consulate. You have applied for a visa to our country and I have a few questions I need to ask." The heavy Afrikaner accent reminded me of State President P.W. Botha. The guy was mildly arrogant right from the start.

"Sure. What would you like to know?" I replied.

"You are (*he paused*) media?" He also punctuated "media" like it was a vulgar word. I explained that I was in fact media. I had clearly stated that when I submitted my application for the visa. There was another pause, probably for him to write it down somewhere. "What is the nature of your visit?" There wasn't an ounce of smile in his voice. I could only wonder how it must feel to be interrogated by their police, every bit as arrogant and no doubt more brutal. I explained the nature of my visit in detail.

He followed up that question by asking if I, "fully understood the current situation in our country?" I assured him that I did. His next question literally caused me to laugh out loud, not a good thing when trying to obtain a visa.

"Upon your return to the U.S., what do you plan to say about our country?"

Once I regained my composure, I answered in a tone as arrogant as his "How can I tell you that when I haven't BEEN to your country?" There was stone cold silence on the other end. I figured he must be writing some serious shit about me at this point. The conversation ended with him snapping, "Thank you sir, that's all I need for now." Click. With that, I was convinced there would be no visa in my foreseeable future. A full six months after I applied, the visa arrived in the mail, stamped for a visit of two weeks.

Life does play its games. During that six month period a number of obstacles presented themselves, each delaying my progress. The Philadelphia radio station where I was working was sold, and the entire staff, including myself, was terminated. Without a job, there was no money for a trip, no need for a visa.

Mandela to be Released? Headlines and stories in the Philadelphia newspapers reflected newspapers from around the world. Was this legitimate or simply the latest round of false hope? Tongues really started to wag when in February 1989 State President P.W. Botha stepped down from leadership after having suffered a stroke the month before. Stubbornly, he held on to the Presidency. The extent of his influence was about but nil by this point. Mandela, Botha, ANC, South Africa, all making the news week after week. What about *Amandla?* Friends and co-workers would ask the same question each time they saw a story about South Africa, "how's the program idea coming?" As they say in South Africa, "Eish." Let's just say my hopes for the demo didn't go according to plan.

The demo was sent to the programming brass at National Public Radio in Washington D.C. This national network of radio stations is *Liberal Central*. If there is a left leaning cause or struggle, NPR is certain to be on the side of the downtrodden. They do their best to be objective, but there is no hiding their liberal sensibilities. To me, NPR was an obvious choice to broadcast my program. Several weeks later I received a call from one of the programming staff informing me that NPR found the program to be "very impressive, but we already have an African show…Afropop."

This was a one-hour program that featured music from the entire continent with virtually no explanation or context. He went on to tell me that I should lose the obvious "political, pro-ANC slant" that the program carried. "Just concentrate on the music" was his final recommendation. Later while relating this to an NPR insider I had come to know, he told me that they were fearful of "pissing off some of their biggest corporate sponsors, because many were still heavily invested in South Africa." How's that for supporting the downtrodden? Ironically, a few years later, NPR and Afropop would approach me to write numerous radio programs about South African music and culture, as well as provide them with contact sources for various news stories. Out the demo goes again, this time to American Public Radio, another national and liberal radio network, not quite as large as NPR, but still an important outlet. They "loved the show" but passed, fearing that "we'd be accused of *copying* Afropop."

Freedom

As my initial dream of a national audience on public radio evaporated, I repeated that Zulu word more and more for inspiration, *Qinisela!* I also learned another great struggle word from my tutor Godfrey, *Phambili!* (Forward). Considering my diminishing options for the program, and getting settled in a new job at another Philadelphia radio station, pretty much took up the remaining months of 1989. All the while records and cassettes continued to flow in from South Africa as well as significant news. P.W. Botha resigned as State President, and F.W. de Klerk assumed the role, while Mandela release rumors jumped in to high gear. Rumors grew to such a fever pitch even the radio DJ's in Philadelphia started talking about Mandela and playing *Sun City, Graceland,* and Peter Gabriel's *Biko* on an increasing rotation. It was the only bit of rock and roll dealing with South Africa and they wanted to play *something* to sound like they were in touch.

As the New Year arrived, so did the realization that I had been working on the project for over two years with no takers. Armed with my demo, a wealth of information and the blessings of the African National Congress, I chose my final target just weeks before an historic announcement an ocean away. It was now or never. "The Voice of the African American Community". That was the slogan of 105.3 WDAS-FM in Philadelphia, the city's number one radio station. With over one millions black residents in the Philadelphia metropolitan area, WDAS, both AM and FM, were indeed powerful voices in the community, and one of the most successful black owned radio groups in all the country.

Why I hadn't thought of approaching them earlier I will never know. Finally I did.

A call was made to the station's Program Manager, Butterball. Yes, the man was on the hefty side, thus Butterball, or simply Butter. I gave him a basic overview of my idea and he agreed to set up a meeting with the General Manager Kernie Anderson and News Director E. Steven Collins to hear my pitch. Walking through the doors of the station for the first time was like walking in to a sacred temple. As a teen I listened to WDAS in two very different incarnations. First, in the late 1960s, it was what people back then called "an underground radio station." Hendrix, Cream, Joplin, Doors, I heard them and more on "WDAS-FM One Nation Underground". WDAS-AM was where *soul* hits would spin day and night. The Temptations, Stevie Wonder, James Brown, Diana Ross. Smokey Robinson, Patti LaBelle. If it had *soul* it was on WDAS-AM. That's where Butterball got his start on the air.

In the early 1970s the FM station changed formats, adopting the much more successful R & B and Soul programming of the AM. Even though I had been working in Philadelphia radio for some time, I had never met anyone from WDAS, and I confess to being a bit star-struck as I entered Butter's office. The walls were covered floor to ceiling with gold records and photos of every super star soul artist imaginable, and Butter knew them all!

As we shook hands, I remembered a high school argument with a fellow student who bragged that black DJs were much better than white DJs, "the brothers are hipper in every way" she said. "Like Butterball, that brother is awesome!" When I told her that Butterball was white, that he just *sounded* black, she snapped "You're full of shit, that's a brother on the radio!" The next day I brought in a piece of promotional material from WDAS featuring the pictures of all of their DJs. There, halfway down the page, was a chubby, white face with the name "Butterball" beneath it. Try and remember this little bit of trivial nonsense for later in the book. Now, here I was, another white guy trying to make a difference with black South African music on a black owned American radio station. Kernie and E. Steven Collins, or E as he was called came in to join us, and I was off like a rocket. "This is a pivotal moment in history" I told them. "Mandela will be released and WDAS can tell the story like no other station in America."

I had all of the pieces in place; the music, the live report, the ANC and we were ready to go. To allay their fears that the African-American community might not take kindly to a white American telling an African story, I offered to write the program and have any announcer of their choosing, preferable an African-American one, host the program. There was a brief pause; I waited, holding my breath in anticipation. They looked at one another as if to see who agreed or objected to my suggestion. Then, the station's General Manager Kernnie turned to E and said "Well?" E smiled and said "there isn't anyone who knows the music, politics or people as well as you do, if we do it…we want YOU as the host."

If they do it? If? It wasn't a "no"; it was "we'll think about it." Then a brief announcement changed the course of history, and many lives, including my own.

'I am now in a position to announce that Mr. Nelson Mandela will be released at the Victor Verster Prison on Sunday, Feb. 11, 1990, at about 3 o' clock, We would all like Mr. Mandela's release to take place in a dignified and orderly manner." FW de Klerk.

It was only a few hours after Nelson Mandela stepped out of prison that my phone rang. It was Butter from WDAS; they wanted the program on the air next Sunday. He went on to say "we're going to do this one show and see how it goes." They were also working on getting a special guest to sit in with me. He wouldn't tell me who that might be. Special guest? I didn't give it a second thought; I was simply ecstatic to think that the program will finally be heard, even if it was just this once.

As I re-joined lovers of freedom everywhere celebrating the release of Mandela, and watched his garage at 8115 Orlando West-Soweto get a fresh coat of black, green and gold paint, I was busy formulating ideas for the magical Sunday that was to come. First, the music; what do I play? If you love music, you probably feel the same excited anticipation I feel as you hurriedly open a new recording. You can't wait to give it a first listen and discover that special track that reaches out and grabs hold of your heart and soul.

Imagine my dilemma then; for years I had been receiving LPs and cassettes and some CDs filled with music that totally captured me. Week after week I found myself elated thanks to the new music that arrived from artists I had never heard of before. The Soul Brothers, Stimela, Brenda Fassie, Mahlathini, Bayete, Amaqabane, Mango Groove, African Jazz Pioneers, Sipho Mabuse. Then I'd be disappointed because I couldn't share it with listeners. Choosing a few tracks for this single, one-hour program seemed an impossible task.

The list was long and styles were as diverse as the nation itself. This required much thought and plenty of listening. During the days leading up to the broadcast Sipho and I discussed the nature of his live report, *Mandela Mania* of course. Meanwhile, *Citizen* Mandela was spending his first week of freedom meeting family and renewing old friendships, while South Africa and the world continued to bask in the glow of this hopeful new dawn. Certainly everyone knew there were troubled times ahead and that more blood was bound to be shed, but for now, for this one moment in time, hope and joy carried the day. Prep and more prep. Butterball phoned on the Friday before the broadcast to tell me that they had secured my *Special Guest;* it was world-renowned South African musician Hugh Masekela! If I had to tell you about Hugh's unequaled contribution to the world of jazz; that, my friends who take a book unto itself. Suffice it to say, he is legendary. As for Sipho's part in this first and possibly only program, one of the most important aspects of his report was logistical, meaning finding a reliable phone.

Sipho lives in the township of Vosloorus, just south-east of Johannesburg, and as hard as it may be to believe in this age of texting, Skype, Smart-Phones, Vonage and more, the vast majority of the township had no phone service in 1990. Mobile phones were years away from becoming commonplace. Often I would contact Sipho at the home of a friend who had phone service. Sometimes the phone service worked, sometimes it didn't. There was never any guarantee. The plan that offered the greatest chance for our having a successful connection was for him to go to his office in the city at a pre-arranged time, in this case, 11:00 am in the states, 6:00 pm in Jo'burg. The music was selected, Sipho was excited, Hugh Masekela was coming and I was running on virtually no sleep and a full load of adrenalin.

The drive from my home in Wilmington, Delaware to just outside of Philadelphia, where most of the city's radio stations are located, takes about an hour and thirty minutes on a workday. Since my wife had a great job in Wilmington, I thought it unfair of me to put the driving burden on her, so we stayed put and I did the long commute to Philly. Listening to the radio, cassette tapes or just having a good *think* passed the time.

If you factored in bad weather, say heavy rain, add an additional thirty minutes to the drive. Put a few inches of snow on the ground and we're talking three hours or more. My record commute was in a February snowstorm, taking nearly ten hours to get home. It was on a Friday, I didn't want to be stuck in Philly for the weekend, so it was push on at all costs. Crazy. This was my commuting routine five days a week. Little did I know that a sixth day would soon be added, and that the routine would continue for years and years.

9:00am Sunday morning, February 18th, 1990. Armed with a stack of LPs, a few CDs, notes and headphones, I hit the road for WDAS-FM. Luckily, the weather that day was spectacular; sunny and warm; nothing remotely like the snowstorm February I mentioned. Heading north through the suburbs, past shopping malls and the schools that once shipped their white students to the inner city, I used the hour-plus drive to play the program out in my head. What I couldn't incorporate into my rehearsal was Hugh Masekela's input. What if he was put off by this white guy doing the program? Who could blame him? Sure, Mandela and the ANC talked about a *non-racial* South Africa, but it had only been one week since his release, and white people were the ones who put him in prison! Nerves kicked in a bit. Shortly before turning down the driveway to WDAS, I calmed myself by remembering the support I was receiving from Godfrey, Sipho, Johnny and others.

They knew and appreciated that my dedication to the struggle was real. Plus, after nearly three years of study, I knew my shit; the history, politics, music, and the language. Okay, maybe not so much the language. I spoke Zulu like a 3 year old, but I *was* learning. As I entered the station I was greeted by more people than I had expected to find on a Sunday morning. Kernie, Butterball, E, Godfrey, his wife Sibongile, whom I hadn't met before, their young daughter Ayanda, members of the news staff and few others I didn't know. No, they weren't here to meet me, it was all for Hugh Masekela who hadn't shown up yet. E was on the air doing his public affairs program and talked up this exciting *special program* about South Africa airing right after his program ended at 11 o'clock. Still, no Hugh to be seen. After the final minutes of E's program I took the chair behind the mic. My first track was ready to play; I loaded the program's introduction into the tape player and at exactly 11 o'clock I hit the play button. *"Amandla!"* was the shout the listeners heard followed by the instrumental track *O Nketsang* by Rex Rabanye, great as a talk over bed. Just as I was introducing myself, and explaining the purpose of the program, into the studio walks Hugh followed by all of the people who had met me at the door when I arrived.

Wearing a black leather jacket and cap, and looking *very* much like Hugh Masekela, he sat down at the guest mic. As I introduced him and we made eye contact it was as clear as the February sky that he was checking me out, probing before validation would be offered. I fully understood and accepted the initial suspicion. That would happen often with other South Africans in the years ahead. I welcomed it. Introductions completed, it was time for music.

The first track, *Chant of the Marching* was from Hugh's friend, and a star in his own right, Sipho "Hotstix" Mabuse. A powerful song, it speaks of *fire and insurrection,* but also of the hope that *"children will learn from our past."* The CD had recently been released in the U.S., but thanks to its ability to paint a vivid picture of oppression, the track was banned in South Africa. The song fades with the sounds of stomping feet and chanting freedom fighters, before a somber verse of *Nkosi Sikelel' iAfrika* brings the song to an emotion end. During the song, Hugh and I talked about Sipho Mabuse and the other artists I intended to play. Stimela, Johnny Clegg, Bayete, Peto, Brenda Fassie. All except Clegg, were new to American ears, but loved by South Africans. As we talked he went through the box of music I had brought. It was during this exchange that Hugh's body language and expression brighten. Right then, I knew he had accepted me along with the purpose of the program. On the air we talked about *protest* songs in South Africa and the pressures artists feel to produce meaningful songs.

Hugh explained, "the truth is, there's hardly any artist I know who started off as an activist musician. I think it takes a slow awakening. It is really like a phenomenon that was broken out after 1976. When all those children were shot in the back, the protest song became more popular with artists." We covered his thoughts on Mandela's release. "To a certain extent I think he surprised and disappointed the European population of South Africa."

He was growing more animated as he continued, "They expected to see a weak old man with a walking stick saying *"okay I'm battered, I give up; I'm ready to compromise."* But when he came out he said *"Listen, if you thought I was bad when you put me in, sit down because you're in for a surprise…are you ready to boogie with this!"* The studio, now overflowing with staff and guests, burst into laughter. From the first five minutes to the final goodbye, the phone lines glowed like a Christmas tree. Hugh and I took call after call from listeners saying pretty much the same thing, "Where has this music been?" Or, "Can I find these songs here in the Philly?" And the most frequently asked, "When will the show be on again?" That question made the efforts of the past several years worthwhile. Sipho came on live from Johannesburg, yes, the phone lines worked perfectly, and he brought us up to date on the excitement that continued to sweep through the nation.

"From townships to rural areas to the big cities" Sipho reported, "There is a sense that real hope for the future has come to South Africa."

Hugh and I continued our exchange of thoughts and ideas about various artists, politics and culture when he suddenly paused, showed a broad smile, turned to Kernie Anderson and laughingly asked, "Where did you get this white boy from the townships? He knows more about South African music than I do!" Kernie was beaming. He knew we had something special. I knew the program was a go! As the hour came to an end, Hugh offered his thoughts for the future, "Hopefully, with all the help we've gotten from everybody, we'll probably see you soon in Pretoria when we go to rename that town. Don't forget to bring your dancing shoes." This was the first, of what would be many programs brought to a close with *Nkosi Sikelel' iAfrika.* It was a good day.

Phambili

The next several months of Mandela's freedom were set to a dizzying pace. His now famous *World Tour* kicked off just two months after his release. As with any rock star or movie idol, everyone wanted to see him, meet him and praise him. In cities throughout Europe and all across the United States, Mandela drew strong support, both moral and financial for the ANC and the vision of a democratic, non-racial South Africa. Back at home, the ANC began to push the foot-dragging government hard for substantive talks, while violence between the ANC and the primarily Zulu based Inkatha Freedom Party began to escalate. The euphoria was fading, and quickly. To fully explain the reasons behind the hatred and mistrust that resulted in this violence requires more than a few lengthy books; therefore, a thumbnail version will have to suffice here. Founded in 1975, Inkatha is led by the Premier of the KwaZulu Natal region Chief Mangosuthu Buthelezi. Having resigned from the ANC to form Inkatha, Buthelezi was seen as a government collaborator and thus despised by ANC supporters. For many of the Zulu people, especially those in rural areas, Inkatha and Buthelezi were symbols of their Zulu culture and pride. Many Zulus felt that the ANC was dominated by members of the rival Xhosa people, who came from the west, in the Transkei region. Once Mandela was released and the ANC unbanned, Buthelezi was worried that he, his party and his people would be marginalized if and when elections took place. Clashes between supporters of the two parties were initially centered in the KwaZulu-Natal region.

However, rouge agents from the apartheid police and army soon saw an opportunity to expand the violence to townships around Johannesburg, and thus destabilize any attempt for unity between the two parties. This third force element, created by these opportunistic members of the police and military, began to arm and even assist members of Inkatha, the majority being migrant workers who had come to Johannesburg. It didn't take long for killings to be followed by revenge killings and so forth. Each new dawn in the townships revealed the carnage from the previous night, and the government offered nothing more than lip service, with no real attempt to stop it.

On the other side of the world in Philadelphia, the audience for the radio program was growing rapidly. Several newspapers published articles highlighting its unique nature and purpose, which helped to push the weekly listenership to well over one-hundred thousand. One reporter asked me about the status of the cultural boycott against South Africa. It was a question that prompted me to invite one of my most valued supporters to join me on the program, The Director of the ANC's Department of Arts and Culture, Barbara Masekela. In short order Barbara made it perfectly clear. "The cultural boycott was never intended to victimize the already victims of apartheid. The cultural boycott is directed at apartheid South Africa." She went on to add, "We are trying to emphasize to the international community that everything should be done to support culture in South Africa of the oppressed people."

When asked how this affects foreign artists who wish to come and help, Barbara laid out the protocol, "At the invitation of democratic cultural organizations, and for the specific purpose of furthering the struggle which is not yet over, these artists can come to assist in the process of building a new South Africa." This was a shift in the party's attitude considering the strong criticism leveled at Paul Simon and even the South African musicians who worked with him such as Ray Phiri, Bakithi Kumalo and others.

Love it or hate, the mass democratic movement had to admit that *Graceland* did South Africa a world of good. Even Barbara's big brother Hugh said "musicians don't start out being political; they are drawn in to it." On one other occasion Hugh was a little more *street* when he told me "musicians don't give a fuck about politics, we're musicians first." Barbara closed with a warning to artists whose motives might be less than admirable, "Because a lot of people are commercially minded, they should come in only with the approval and in consultation with the democratic movement." In a matter of a few months, Barbara would take on a new role in the ANC, but that's for later.

The music, interviews, and information were fast becoming learning tools for Americans; while Sipho also served as a lifeline to home for the large number of South Africans living in the greater Philadelphia area.

Unknown to me at first, Sipho had made a significant career move. In a conflict which stemming from his participation with the radio program, he resigned as editor of Jive magazine and set out on his own. Due to his dedication to *Amandla!* several opportunities that might have been open to him…were suddenly closed. Being the good man that he is, he never told me of the hardships he endured until years later. Since the majority of the music was unavailable in the states, I urged listeners to record the program. A fair number of them began sending copies to friends and family in other parts of the world. Letters from South Africa, Zimbabwe, Zambia, even Australia came to the station singing its praises and asking if it can be heard in their country. Humbling.

All of us were thrilled with the positive response. The South African record labels were thrilled with the feedback from listeners as well. Finally, their artists had a platform to be heard and I urged them to release more music in the states. Mango Groove's label took the positive response to heart and released their first South African LP here in the states. I was asked to consult with the US label about the release. Do *not* tamper with Mango Groove's unique style of Marabi jazz and penny whistle Kwela music was my plea. This was music born in township shebeens and on the street corners of Johannesburg in the forties and fifties, and given a modern twist by the band.

In the early summer months of our first year, Brenda Fassie's label phoned to tell me that an American label was keen to release her music in the US. This was great news. Again, I was asked to consult with track selection, I was honored to do so. Since the 1980s, Brenda was a bona-fide super star in South Africa. Her infectious African-Pop style was copied by numerous imitators-yet none of them could ever come close to her immense star-power. A few weeks later the label informed me that they were bringing Brenda to the states and to Philly to do the program.

My wife and I picked her up along with the label executive at the Philly train station. Dressed in a beautiful blue dress adorned with African embroidery and floral headscarf, the very petite Brenda was a dynamo and I couldn't wait to get her behind the mic! We opened the program with her hit *Jail to Jail* and Brenda sang *live* along with it. Awesome. Since he and Brenda went back a long way, I brought Sipho on from Jo'burg to join the conversation. His first question to her was, "How are you liking the *re-mix* they have done to *Black President?*" Brenda's now classic tribute to Nelson Mandela was given a very, *western* dance groove. It sounded a continent apart from the brilliant South African original. With the label executive sitting just to her right, a hesitant Brenda asked, "Am I free to say my feelings?" The answer was "yes." She continued, "I am worried that people won't understand the song unless they read the lyrics. The American version is too disco-ized Sipho, and I feel the message is losing its strength."

She put it plainly, "The American version, I really don't like it, let me be truthful." At my urging, the label did include the original as a bonus track. Ever the self-promoter, Brenda used a sales pitch from a US news article written by a misinformed reporter. "I hate talking about this, because I don't like to talk about myself" she said, "but I am the niece of Mandela."

She continued telling a sort of half-truth, "He and I are of the same clan, the Madiba clan, and if I want to marry, I have to get his permission." This connection to Mandela was exploited in a press release from the record label, and of course by Brenda. One could hardly blame her, the U.S. was new territory and selling copies of her CD meant doing some hawking. We opened the phone lines to listeners and calls of praise from American and South Africa listeners flooded in. A few South African callers and Brenda were in tears as they spoke of home and the hope for the new South Africa. It was a very emotional program for all of us.

A great boost to the program came when the internationally acclaimed, Emmy award winning TV program *South Africa Now* featured a story on *Amandla!* I had put them in touch with Brenda's record label in hopes they would air the new video for *Black President,* which they did, and subsequently brought a film crew to Philly to do the story on the program. Additional press came our way thanks to a connection of Sipho's. The legendary South African newspaper The Sowetan ran a nice feature article highlighting our efforts in the states; although it did downplay the political nature of the program and its ANC leaning host.

It was the definitive news magazine for anyone interested in South Africa. For our feature, they sent a free-lance video crew in Johannesburg to Sipho's office to shoot *him* as he spoke to *me* live. The result allowed our listeners to get a real feel for how the program evolved and was being produced. It gave me, the white guy doing a program on South Africa, an even higher level of credibility. The producer of the segment did ask me to remove my ever-present ANC lapel pin. She said, "While we fully support the ANC, we don't want to alienate the other anti-apartheid organizations." I understood and willingly obliged.

Additional press came our way thanks to a connection of Sipho's. The legendary South African newspaper *The Sowetan* ran a nice feature article highlighting our efforts in the states; although it did downplay the political nature of the program and its ANC leaning host. Even the government controlled South African Broadcasting Corporation conducted a live radio interview with me early one morning. The presenters were intrigued that a white American had such a deep interest and understanding of South African music. They fired off several fluff questions "How?" "What's your favorite group?" and "Have you been to South Africa?" Boring shit. To spice things up, I mentioned my strong support for culture's role in the struggle and for the ANC. At that, the interview came to an immediate end. "Thanks James and good luck." That was fun.

I was constantly reading books on South African history, bios, news reports and more, in addition to studying isiZulu with help from my tutors Godfrey and Sibongile. No doubt my childlike fluency had them both in stitches at times. Sibongile had a grand laugh when I asked her if she was *cooking* the children, and not *watching* them. South Africans on both sides of the ocean gleefully observed, "you speak Zulu with an American accent." Mild teasing aside, they were full of sincere encouragement as I pressed on. My studies were usually carried out during my nearly three-hour, to and from daily commute to my *bill-paying* job at the radio station. The dashboard would be covered with yellow sticky notes containing ten new words every day. Imagine doing fifty to sixty miles an hour while trying to read *sebenza* (work), *siza* (help), *khumbula* (remember). I am surprised this method of learning didn't result in *ingozi* (accident).

The long commutes were also the perfect opportunity to review new releases sent from South Africa. Combine it all with endless faxes, middle of the night phone calls; seems my friends and contacts in Jo'burg never got the time difference thing worked out, plus extensive research, and it was little wonder that the program consumed me 24/7. This state of total *consumption* was such that for the first half of 1991, significant news events involving the U.S. that should have taken center stage in my brain, simply didn't. Operation Desert Storm being the elephant in the room, the brutal beating of Rodney King at the hands of the Los Angeles police, which later would spark massive riots, the *official* reunification of Germany, and Queen Elizabeth II addresses the U.S. Congress. Okay, that one was *easily* ignored.

My attention, as well as Sipho's and the South African community in the Philadelphia area, was focused on the slaughter of forty people at a night vigil in Sebokeng by members of Inkatha. This was followed by the fifteen mourners also murdered by Inkatha in Alexandra Township at a night vigil. We watched with fragile hope as Mandela, de Klerk and Buthelzi held *peace* talks amidst the bloodshed. Many were shaken when Winnie Madikizela-Mandela was found guilty and sentenced to six years for her involvement in the death of 14-year old Stompie Moeketesi. All of this drama, violence and despair coming within eighteen months after Mandela's euphoric walk to freedom. Bloody, hopeful, sad, whatever the news, Sipho brought it to the listeners.

The program's cultural mission continued to be fulfilled through interviews and music from a wide array of talented artists including The Soul Brothers with their infectious brand of organ based *mbaqanga* and sweet vocals. Composer Moses Ngwenya expressed amazement at their popularity outside of South Africa. "Although we had that dream that one day we would be stars, we are *very* surprised by our popularity in Europe and now in the U.S. because people can't even understand the words to our songs since they are sung in Zulu."

Exiled jazz legend Jonas Gwangwa joined me to talk about his music as well as serving as Musical Director for the ANC's traveling cultural program *Amandla,* during the '80s. "We put together a show, with music, poetry and dancing to give the international community an idea of what is happening in South Africa. It's a show done in documentary style telling the story of South Africa from pre-colonial days, touching on the highlights of the struggle." As Director, Jonas chose to leave the audience uplifted at the conclusion. "Because the story of South Africa is a tragic story, we end the show with a medley of traditional dances from the different ethnic groups, so we end up with a high." He also shared stories of his home coming concert in South Africa. "It was overwhelming. Thirty years is a long time. I was worried about making the standard, what people expect of me, the first time performing for my people in thirty years. As an artist, you do have stage fright, but this time it was a little bit more than usual, but I managed."

Having numerous listeners who were fans of African-American poet Gil Scott-Heron, myself included, I was convinced they would love *The People's Poet* Mzwakhe Mbuli. I wasn't wrong. You didn't have to be South African to know that Mzwakhe put in to words what tens of thousands felt. After being cleared of a false charge of possession of a hand grenade, Mzwakhe was given a limited passport to travel to Europe and a few U.S. cities. For obvious reasons, Philadelphia was one of the cities.

"Unfortunately, things are not free at home," Mzwakhe told listeners who were eager to see his live show that week. "I will be happy and glad to see you in a free South Africa. At the moment, I still don't have a vote, but I still create. The Berlin Wall is gone, but apartheid is still there." When asked what to expect at the show, "I will shock the world." Three days later, at a jam packed African music club in West Philadelphia, I brought Mzwakhe and his band on stage to wild cheering and applause. Yes, he *did* shock the world, at least our little part of it.

Thanks to the exposure on the radio program, artists such as Mzwakhe, Johnny Clegg, and Mahlathini and the Mahotella Queens were thrilled to find an audience who knew their music, and came ready for a great time. Artists and audience never went away disappointed. As is the case of traveling musicians, there was never any time to really see Philadelphia or for me to spend more than a few hours with them. Still, virtually every artist who came in to the studio or who joined me on the phone had the same initial reaction best described as quizzical. You could almost hear their thoughts, "How does this white American know so much about South African music? *My* music?" In their own way, each of these amazing people helped expand the program's reach and credibility; but none more than pop star turned struggle music hero Blondie Makhene.

The pop singing duo of brothers Blondie and Pappa Makhene enjoyed super-star status during the first half of what was perhaps the most violent decade in South Africa, the 1980s. As a successful record producer with a keen eye for talent, Blondie is credited with discovering Brenda Fassie. Near the end of the decade the brother duo split, and Blondie moved toward, or was drawn into what he called *struggle* or *toyi-toyi* music. These songs of liberation were sung by freedom fighters and at anti-government rallies throughout South Africa. He formed an instrumental band, African Youth Band, or AYB. Their albums were comprised of instrumental versions of well-known *struggle* songs, Blondie explained to listeners that "we did it this way so that everyone could sing these songs of liberation in their own language." Since these tracks contained no openly anti-government lyrics, they actually got airplay on the government-controlled radio! Crafty bugger that Blondie. To his utter surprise, SABC-TV used one of the band's more popular tracks, *Ntate Modise* for a talk-over bed as Nelson Mandela walked out of prison! A short time later, Blondie morphed the group into something even more militant, calling the group *Amaqabane*, a township term meaning *comrades*. Now, they sang the struggle songs, all of which were immediately banned by the SABC. Of course this made the group even more beloved in the townships and with the ANC. *Amaqabane* was frequently the inspirational entertainment at countless rallies across the country.

Early on Blondie became a long distance friend and an active supporter of the program, providing insight, introductions to ANC members and other musicians. One morning in mid-summer he called to tell me that he had organized for me a fifteen day visit to South Africa courtesy of his label and a few others who believed in what I was doing.

He knew that my lack of funds made it almost impossible for me to get myself there any time soon. When I tried to thank him for this extraordinary gesture, Blondie said, "Comrade, you are doing great work for the oppressed people of South Africa, but you must come to see and talk with the people first hand, then, you will truly understand what is happening." The dates were set. At long last I would visit what had over time become my adopted homeland.

The Journey

It is difficult to review our goodbye at the Philadelphia airport. The sight of my wife's face is still fresh in my mind. Watching Charlottie's brown eyes fill with tears broke my heart. She was certain that death awaited me, and that my going was comparable to my leaving her. As painful as it was for her to let me go, I smile to think that I was going BECAUSE of her. If she wasn't such an amazingly strong and supportive woman, my hopes for the program and my ultimate dream of visiting South Africa would have been scrapped. On many occasions we were told by friends and family that we were "too close for our own good." Facing 15 days away from her, I couldn't help but think how I pitied those people. Not knowing a love such as ours is their loss. As for my flight, I almost missed it. Charlottie and I were so involved in saying goodbye, hugging, crying and kissing; I failed to hear the boarding announcement. For some unknown reason, both of us were struck by the realization that it had grown extremely quiet in the terminal. We looked around and noticed that everyone; and I do mean everyone in the gate area had gone. I rushed to find an attendant and explained the reason for my temporary deafness. With a smile she quickly re-opened the gate for me. Boarding the tiny twin-prop commuter to New York I fought back tears as I spotted Charlottie standing at the terminal window alone and crying. How deeply I love her and how heavy the guilt; yet, we both knew this was a journey that I had to make. The flight to New York was an uneventful one and I was thankful for the thirty-five minutes of quiet reflection.

Once I found the proper international terminal, I was only too happy to put down my two hundred pounds of carry-on baggage and phone Charlottie. She had composed herself and was back at our home with her sister Elizabeth. They were preparing for a vacation trip to Maine, along with my mother and brother. It made me feel a little bit better, but not much.

After a few more loving goodbyes on the telephone, I wheeled my bags to the Sabina terminal and waited. The very thought of having to drag these anchors around two more airports before I could free myself made me ache. Charlottie was kind enough to have picked up a hamburger at 1:00 pm before she drove me to the airport. It was now 7:00 pm and it was time to eat it. Stone cold and flavorless, a condition many would consider normal for such a treat, the burger was consumed while I watched a veritable United Nations parade of passengers before me. Indians, French, Britons, Africans and even a few Afrikaners were scattered here and there. Simply hearing Afrikaans conjured up harsh images of the ultimate in racism. Be my luck I'll be seated with a few of them all the way to Jo'burg. My imagination began to run wild with our in-flight conversation...

"Have you ever been to South Africa?" They'll ask in that smiling, investigative tone of theirs. I know it's terribly unfair to brand every Afrikaner a paranoid racist, but past experience had taught me that behind that smile, there's only one thing they really want to know; just how aware are you of the "situation in our country?"

My imaginary exchange continued, "No, this is my first trip and I'm really looking forward to it." My enthusiasm will convince them that I must be going to visit family or friends, white friends of course. "Oh, are you going to Jo'burg to visit friends?" again with that phony smile. "Sort of, most of my friends live in the townships." This time, I'll do the smiling. In my estimation once I tell them how I'm working with the ANC our conversation will either cease or come to a boil.

As I'm mulling over the make-believe possibilities, my flight to Brussels is called. This flight, like the one to New York was without incident. Not one big bump to cause panic, and no Afrikaner to argue with. The only problem was a seat that refused to stay "in the full upright position." It was 6 full hours in which to contemplate all that awaited me in South Africa and all that I was leaving behind at home. We arrived in Brussels sometime around 8:00 a.m. As a gesture of thanks for flying Sabina, I was given a coupon good for a free breakfast. I didn't sleep a minute on the plane, and ate nothing; perhaps I'll give it a go. So, with my two tons of carry-on beside me, it seemed heavier at this point, I boarded the moving sidewalk in search of my bounty. After what seemed like a few hundred miles, I stepped off into the main concourse and located the restaurant. There I discovered something I'd never seen before, rows and rows of tables filled with dozens of people all drinking beer…at 8:00 a.m. Was Belgium famous for beer? I had no idea, but I concluded that it must be because these people were gulping it down as if it were liquid gold.

Stepping up nearer to the checkout, I listened closely, trying to ascertain the cashier's linguistic abilities. In other words, I can't speak a word of French and if she doesn't speak English, I guess I won't be eating. Thankfully, she does speak English. I showed her my *valuable* coupon and she kindly explained that I was eligible for a soft drink and one baguette. Great, I know what a soft drink is, but a baguette? I assume it's edible, but is it something I would WANT to eat? Maybe I can wait until the next flight. Trying desperately not to look like the classic unwashed American scum, I calmly glance around at the wide variety of *serve yourself* foods. There are huge platters with sandwiches, fruits and chips, piping hot soups, salads, and burgers. Perhaps my baguette is one of these platters? Maybe it isn't.

Not prepared for any sort of grand embarrassment just yet, I turn to leave. As I do, a rotating display sitting off to the side catches my eye. There, spinning around ever so slowly, sat tiny little sliced croissants, one to a plate. Each contained a single, almost transparent slice of meat between the crunchy halves. Above the display on a petite cardboard sign the word *Baguette*. Ah, my first French lesson. What the hell, I do have a valuable coupon good for a free one, go for it. I tried to assess which of the miniature pastries was the biggest and most packed. After a few minutes of watching them go by again and again, I realized that the person who prepared the freebie baguette was a master of consistency; everyone was exactly the same size with exactly the same amount of meat within it. I grabbed the next one that came by, handed over my coupon and devoured it along with my complimentary, way too warm of a soft drink.

It was 8:20a.m., and with the first part of my journey now complete, I only had 8 more hours to kill. Since the majority of the airport was undergoing total reconstruction, that left only the small aforementioned temporary international terminal to explore. My exploration took all of 5 minutes and included the walk back to the sitting area to await my late afternoon flight to South Africa. I took up a position that enabled me to view the comings and goings of fellow travelers; faces from foreign lands, voices from foreign lands, screaming babies with foreign cries, and announcements in tongues from seemingly every nation...the last being English. The hours crept by as numerous aches in my body grew more pronounced, courtesy of unyielding, molded plastic chairs. There's not much one can say about sitting for 8 hours in a drab airport lounge far from home. The mind drifts into a dream like state, retreating as if to protect itself from the possibility of anxiety. At least *my* mind does.

The hours did pass and finally the multi-linguistic public address system stated that "passengers could now prepare to board Sabina Flight 211 to Kinshasa, Zaire and on to Johannesburg, South Africa." Of course, the English version was the last announcement in the flurry. With bags checked and carry-on in hand I boarded Sabina Flight 211. What luck! I had a seat right next to one of the doors offering miles of legroom! At last I'll be able to recline and perhaps get some sleep. It was nearing 6:00 p.m. Brussels time and I had been awake for twenty-eight hours. Little did I know that would be extended to nearly forty-eight!

Our flight time of twelve hours to Johannesburg would include a stopover in Kinshasa, Zaire to pick up additional food and fuel. Recently, I had read that the political atmosphere in Zaire was heating up. Press reports were using terms like "the potential for civil war" as they detailed the troubles there. What the hell was I getting myself in to? As for my great seat location; the extra legroom was taken up by passengers choosing to stand in front of me and drink themselves silly. Hour after hour passed by, I sat awake and cramped, and thus retreated to that place I described earlier. The highlight of the flight was viewing a violent thunderstorm over Central Africa from thirty thousand feet. Oh, and really great coffee! Lots and lots of it! It was 5:00 a.m. when our flight finally touched down at Jan Smut Airport outside of Johannesburg. In a state of mild exhausting I found my place in the queue, began the slow shuffle down the aircraft aisle, descended the stairs and suddenly felt the exhaustion turn to exhilaration as I set foot on South African soil for the very first time.

As we crossed the tarmac and in to the customs terminal, my mind was filled with rapid-fire images of what may await me. The level of political violence in the townships had escalated to an alarming rate and I couldn't help but wonder; was my wife's concern for my safe return well founded? After all, I would be spending much of my time in the townships.

My thoughts on the matter of my personal safety were interrupted as the first piece of luggage slammed its way onto the baggage carousel. The feeding frenzy had begun. Passengers, who just a few short moments ago were calmly walking single file, were now bumping and jostling each other to retrieve their bags. I stood at a safe distance, deciding it best to allow the frenzy to slow; besides, neither of my bags had made their way on to the carousel. As the pace of the arriving baggage slowed to a trickle and the crowd thinned to just a few, I tried to fight off the fear of lost baggage. My attempts failed when I found myself standing in a now empty terminal watching an empty, rattling carousel go round and round. Believing that I could somehow *will* my bags to appear, I walked up to the gapping mouth of the carousel and fixed my most intense focus directly on it. Nothing. At the very moment that my hopes slid toward resignation, the black hole spit out both of my bags and the clanking carousel came to a sudden stop. This was going to be a very interesting experience.

With bags in hand I headed toward my first encounter with South African authority, Customs. Three agents were working customs that morning, two of which seemed nice enough, smiling, chatting with the arrivals and wishing them a good stay or welcome home. The third was the epitome of everything my vivid imagination had conjured up in regards to an authoritative Afrikaner. Angry face, quick, cutting dialogue and a demeanor which shouted "Don't fuck with me." Please, I thought; let me get a *nice* Boer.

"Next!" shouted the world's most angry man. I was frozen for a moment thinking perhaps he was talking to someone else. "NEXT!!" The shout was even louder this time. Shit, this trip is not going well and I haven't gotten out of the airport. I quickly made my way to the counter and deposited all of my bags for his inspection. "Passport." Clumsily, I handed it over. As he studied my passport he snapped, "Open your bags." I started to open my bags when his tone turned very interrogative. "Media? What are you plans in our country?" No worries, I was prepared for this. Friends in South Africa told me ahead of time, "tell them what they want to hear and move on." Easy enough. "I'm here to interview musicians and artists." Once again he looks at my passport, then at me, then down at my bags, one of which is completely empty. With his eyes fixed right on mine he asks, "Why is this case empty?" His tone had grown suspicious. "I'll be bringing back several recordings, albums and CDs." Which was in fact true. There was what I took to be a deliberate pregnant pause, one designed to make me sweat a bit. I stared straight back into his angry eyes. In a flash he dropped my passport on the counter, slammed the rubber stamp down upon it, handed it to me and in a monotone voice said, "Have a good visit in our country." At last, I was in!

Having been the last to retrieve my bags and the last to clear customs, I was now the last to enter the main terminal...the seemingly empty main terminal. Where was everyone? More importantly, where was Sipho? My journalist friend was supposed to be here. He was supposed to be the first to welcome me to South Africa. Instead, four blue-clad, shotgun-toting members of the South African Police Service (SAPS) were my welcoming committee. They stood chatting in a circle about twenty feet from me and turned in unison to check me out. One said something in Afrikaans, which resulted in all four having a good hearty laugh. Now I was the one getting paranoid. For years I had read, heard about and saw video of horrendous acts of violence against the people of South Africa at the hands of the SAPS, and here they were, right in front of me.

For some reason known only to the designers of this particular terminal, there was no place to sit, not even one of those pain-inducing plastic chairs that I came to know so well in Brussels. With nowhere to sit, I pulled my bags off to the side and waiting for Sipho, determined not to look at all uncomfortable. A half hour of listening to the Afrikaans speaking SAPS was beginning to take its toll, when to my right I heard "Unjani 'Mfowethu!" (*How are you my brother?*) There, at last was Sipho. He looked just as he did in the photos I'd seen of him, his thin frame decked out in a vivid blue *Athletic Club Member* winter jersey, and his face brightened by a moustache-adorned grin stretching ear to ear.

Before I arrived, I had insisted that Sipho speak only Zulu, what better way for me to improve? "Ngiyajabula kakhulu ukukubona Mfowethu!" (*I am very happy to see you my brother*) I responded as we embraced. I made certain to speak loud enough to be heard by the shotgun foursome nearby, who suddenly had fallen mute. As we walked away, Sipho said "Umzodla umyani kufike yini?" Actually, I don't know what the hell he said…it ran together in such a blur. Christ, I was dead on my feet and could barely speak English let alone Zulu! "Please" I said, "Ignore my previous request." Sipho's reply, 'Yebo" (*Yes*), the smartass. We tossed my bags into the back of his fire engine red Ford Fiesta complete with cracked windscreen and intense petro fumes, and headed off toward Sipho's home. Our destination was the township of Vosloorus just southeast of Johannesburg, an area Sipho described as having a "country feel."

At each turn, and around each bend, I felt an overwhelming sensation of comfort. How was it possible that this place could seem so familiar, so much like home? It just felt right. As we rolled in to Vosloorus the images I had come to know only through photos and on television became reality. There were some dusty informal settlements clustered around the perimeter of the township. Informal Settlements, that's the kinder way to describe makeshift shacks thrown together in haphazard confusion.

In other sections, homes took on a more conventional appearance; small, 4 room brick buildings with postage stamp yards, many behind fences and walls; some derelict, still others were spacious and immaculate; desirable homes in any community anywhere. Sipho's *desirable* home was situated behind a high, gated wall, which hid from view about a quarter of an acre of property. The one-story structure had a bit of a Spanish feel, with several large arched windows and tile roof. Sipho was by any standard, a successful professional. He parked the fire engine red Ford, closed the gates and we headed inside. For a moment, I thought how quiet and serene it all seemed in this country setting. The mood was short lived. As a distant rumble grew louder and closer. Sipho called me to the door and said "James, welcome to South Africa." There, just one block over, a caravan of Casspirs and Hippos came rolling in to keep the peace. These are the infamous army and police vehicles seen so many times on the news doing battle with townships residents. Once again, reality took hold as I watched the dust of apartheid oppression rise, and this time it wasn't on TV.

After a light breakfast, and a few hours of finally getting to talk face to face, we made our way to the hotel that Blondie had arranged for me in Johannesburg. All the while I was fighting hard to suppress thoughts of my wife; emotions were already running high in these first few hours. Blondie had told me that some of my kind sponsors wanted to put me up in one of the finest hotels in Johannesburg, away from any trouble spots. Blondie insisted that I stay a little closer to reality-The Protea Garden Hotel, Berea; right on the edge of Hillbrow.

In its heyday, Hillbrow was the Greenwich Village, the Soho of Johannesburg, artsy, very multi-cultural, and vibrant with a dash of danger for good measure. Hillbrow offered all of the excitement that makes the hip part of any city…hip. That was Hillbrow in better days. Now, Sipho tells me that while it still has a mystique, it was rapidly deteriorating into a crime ridden shell of its former self, not as hip and much more dangerous. I couldn't wait to see it. Having grown up in an urban area, I watched my city and others like it decline and rebound and decline again over the years. I wasn't terribly shocked at the look and feel of Johannesburg.

For those who know Johannesburg intimately, I beg that you give me a moment to share a bit of info with those who have never been there, and those who may have no concept of it whatsoever. Johannesburg is a major city, in fact, one of the fifty largest cities in the world. It does not sit in the middle of the jungle. It is not filled with wild Africans carrying spears and shields, and yes, it has electricity. Forgive the sarcasm, but before and after my visit, I was asked these sorts of questions repeatedly. They don't call Africa the *Dark Continent* for nothing. As for Hillbrow and Berea where I'd be staying, there were many multi-storied apartment buildings, once grand, now run down and shabby. Several office buildings stood empty of tenants, perhaps a few windows smashed. All in all it looked identical to the downtown of numerous big cities I had visited.

My hotel stood in the middle of the block, a modest structure of about 10 stories. Like the buildings around it, it had seen better days, but what did I care, I was finally in South Africa and knew I wouldn't be spending much time in my room. As Sipho and I entered the lobby to check me in, I could almost feel the change that came over the white desk clerk. You sure as hell could see it! She looked at Sipho with the utmost suspicion, and when it became obvious that he was my friend, her attitude toward me grew icy cold. That shocked me far more than the look of the surrounding area. Black people were everywhere around Berea, why was she still so…Boer?

After getting checked in by Madame Racist, Sipho headed for home and I headed to my eighth floor, street-side room. Nice enough, brown motif on walls, carpet and bedspread. A TV and a writing desk sat to one side of the room, while a small round table with two chairs occupied space near the window. Of course, brown tablecloth, brown chairs. Who was their decorator? At this point I was running on pure adrenaline and was surprised that I was able to function. I unpacked, actually took time to hang up my clothes hoping to shed the wrinkles, and splashed a little cold water on my face. It was time to call home and let Charlottie know that I was alive and well. Early on in my involvement with South Africans, I was told that due to the nature of my business, being a media-type, an unfriendly media-type at that, my phone calls would certainly be monitored. And so they were.

As Sipho's reports became more and more critical of the government, we experienced a significant increase in mysteriously dropped calls while *live* on the air, with a total inability to reconnect for hours. ANC members in South Africa had told me in no uncertain terms that both my out-going and in-coming calls at the hotel would be monitored. "You'll hear a click and then a slight drop in volume." Their description was spot on. I placed my call through the hotel switchboard and within the first minute of my conversation with my wife…click…and a decrease in volume. I figured if these sorry bastards want to hear me tell my wife that I love and miss her go ahead. The eavesdropping was to continue with every call I made and received during my entire visit. What did I have to say that could possibly be of interest to these assholes? Not long after hanging up from my wife and the curious security branch, there was a knock on the door. It was my friend and sponsor Blondie Makhene along with his four beautiful daughters ages 4 to 13. Blondie was pure energy bouncing in to hug me. "James E-OP-OH-LOW…welcome home Com!" His long braids were tied behind his head, and his smile and eyes beamed with delight. I had to smile at his Martin Luther King "I Have a Dream" T-shirt. They had come to collect me for my first day of adventure. I didn't tell them that I hadn't slept since Thursday. Off we went.

Blondie's wife Agnes was waiting in their kombi, a mini-bus adorned with the names of his labels top artists. Blondie Makhene, Amaqabane, Pure Gold, and Platform One, We climbed in and were off for a tour of Jo'burg. They pointed out all sorts of landmarks that I had read about for years. Now, here they were. Some famous for music, theatre, politics, some infamous such as the John Vorster Square police station where many suspected enemies of the state were held in detention, often tortured and where some supposedly jumped from the 10th floor.

It was going on late afternoon when we headed to Blondie's home in Fluerhof, a suburb of Johannesburg populated by upwardly mobile black and so-called colored professionals. These were three and four bedrooms homes with beautiful tile roofs, whitewashed walls, in-ground pools and high fences and walls. "How" I asked "were blacks and coloreds able to swing this?" Blondie chuckled, "This used to be all white" he said. Then, he pointed over the rooftops and said, "See over there, just beyond that field?" I looked in the direction his was pointing. "That my brother, is Soweto, and when it started growing too close, all the white people moved out and WE moved in!" He let out a huge infectious laugh. Blondie's house was bustling with activity outside and inside. Several tables and chairs along with coolers of beer and sodas were placed around the pool. Inside, women were busily cooking away in the kitchen. "We're having a braai (*cookout*) in your honor" Agnes said. "Many of the people who brought you here are coming!"

By dusk the house was packed, and so was the area around the pool. After years of phone calls and faxes, I finally got to meet some of the record executives who had been supporting my efforts. Musicians came; neighbors came, both from Fluerhoff and from too close for white people's comfort, Soweto. One invited guest wasn't a stranger to me at all; it was South African superstar Brenda Fassie. We had spoken on the phone a few times about a month before my arrival in South Africa and even talked about her first appearance on my program. Blondie greeted her with a hug and said "Sis, you remember James?" Through eyes as glassy as marbles Brenda stared straight at me and slurred, "I'm very pleased to meet you." Almost shouting in her face Blondie interjects "Fuck Brenda, you were just with James in Philadelphia!" Brenda struggled hard to refocus her drug-glazed eyes on me, then, pulled back as if someone had stuck her with a pin. "Oh shit, James, how are you my brother?" I was happy that she recognized me, but sad to see that she was so incredibly stoned. She introduced me to her current boyfriend and the two of them staggered inside to find a drink. Flashing forward, Brenda would experience major drug and health related setbacks, dying as a result in 2004.

Throughout the evening I was repeatedly, but kindly interrogated by Blondie's guests. Like Hugh Masekela before them, they wanted to trust me, but needed to be certain that I deserved their trust. Again and again I explained my program and my beliefs, once satisfied that I was sincere, the floodgates to their stories fell open.

Thembi, whose sister was dragged from a taxi by a roving band of Inkatha thugs and hacked to death. She was so frightened when they stopped the taxi that she forgot to speak Zulu and spoke Xhosa instead, a sure sign that you must be an ANC supporter.

Vusi, who had spent months in detention without being charged and was repeatedly tortured by the police, released, only to be re-arrested and the cycle start over again.

Simon, who was living in one of the informal settlements called Zonke Zizwe (all nations), when members of Inkatha broke into his shack, held his left hand down on the table and ordered him to sign membership in Inkatha with the right hand…or have the left chopped off.

Thando, who just the night before, had gone to her sister's home to help with a domestic problem. The police arrived and arrested everyone. They placed Thando, along with her ten year-old son in the back of a police van. When she protested, explaining that she was simply trying to help her sister, a policeman threw a tear gas grenade in to the van, nearly choking them to death. Her son had to be rushed to the hospital after they were released.

The stories went on and on. Once the bond between us was established, they were seizing this opportunity to tell their story to someone on the *outside*. Even with all the pain in their voices and in their stories, each meeting ended with either a heartfelt handshake or hug and big smiles. Blondie was right; I had to see the people, talk to the people, to fully understand.

At one point, I found myself sitting on the floor in one of the bedrooms surrounded by *young lions* from Soweto. These are young men who basically have had enough shit from the government, and fail to see any advantage to non-violent change. They are disciplined, but also ready to light the fuse if needs dictate; we were joined by Liz, an executive from one of the major record labels.

They were doing their interrogation when Liz, who is *colored,* shouted at me. "Why do you call the show Amandla? Why a Zulu word?" I completely understood her anger at my choice of a name for the program. The violence between the ANC and the Zulu based Inkatha Freedom Party was costing hundreds of lives, so many in fact, that Mandela, Zulu leader Buthelezi and President de Klerk signed a Peace Accord that very day. It was supposed to end violence between the ANC and Inkatha, as well as curtail the *third force* and police violence. Considering the number of bodies that would continue to stack up, it was and remains debatable whether it did any good at all. The result of this growing level of Inkatha against the ANC violence meant that many people, like Liz, branded all Zulu people as government sponsored terrorists. I started to explain my reasoning when Liz laid in to me again. "That's a Zulu word man! Why not Xhosa or Sotho? Don't you know what they are doing?"

Just then, Blondie rushed in to intervene. I told him things were fine and not to worry. "Liz, listen" I said. "I chose Amandla because it means *power*...power in the music...power in the voice of the people. Beside, it's a Xhosa word as well and it's shouted at every anti-apartheid rally in South Africa. MY people, the people I am trying to educate KNOW the word already. They already understand its importance. That is why I chose it." I could see the light come on in her brain...Liz finally got it and apologized for offending me. Apologize? This is South Africa, people were being brutally murdered on trains, in taxis and on the streets of townships every day and night, and she is apologizing to me?

 It was going on midnight when one of my record label supporters offered to take me back to my hotel. I said my goodbyes, collapsed in the back seat of the car and we headed for the hotel. Back in my room, my head went spinning with voices, images, music, projections of what tomorrow might bring and the expectation of Charlottie's call to me at 3 a.m. South Africa time. I was able to get maybe an hour and a half of sleep. My emotions were running wild as I tried to put into words what I had just experienced. Of course, the eavesdroppers were on the line as well. Don't these people have lives? It's 3 a.m. for Christ's sake!

We talked for over a half hour with the majority of the conversation being "I love you, I miss you." We said goodbye and I flipped on the TV and watched "The Natural" starring Robert Redford, a great baseball movie. There was no way I could sleep. I saw the first of what would be 14 hotel room dawns. This would be the pattern of my entire stay in Johannesburg. Picked up early, dropped off very late, a little sleep, a 3 a.m. phone call, watch a movie, watch the dawn, and start all over.

Soweto

Early morning, and my tour guide, Blondie Makhene is here to collect me. Today it's the Southwest Township, aka Soweto. Naturally, he's driving the KGM (his record label) kombi. Hey, if you're going in to the center of your fan base, you want to be seen. That being said, I confess to having mixed feelings about our mode of transport. On one hand, people in the townships love Blondie; he's a music star and pro ANC. When they see his kombi they'll be thrilled to see us. On the flipside, the kombi is painted in ANC colors…black, green and gold; a perfect target for Inkatha supporters. What the hell, I happily climb in. Before heading to Soweto, we first make a stop at Blondie's office to pick up three of his best friends. Vusi, another popular singer on Blondie's label, burly in stature and quiet by nature. MK, who as a young boy in March, 1960, accompanied his grandfather to Sharpeville to protest the hated passbook system and witnessed 59 people massacred by police. Dressed in shirt and tie, MK was skipping work to join us. He was all smiles and funny as hell. The last of our party was Connie, gregarious, witty, and dressed in a New York Yankees pinstripe jersey and cap, Connie is full of hope for his 6-year-old twin boys. They all wanted to be part of my Soweto indoctrination.

The highway leading in to Soweto is extremely wide and well maintained; it was designed that way they tell me, to make it easy for troops to get in quickly. "Most of the streets are shit once you get in deep" says MK. In we go.

First stop, Diepkloof. Just as we were entering this eastern section of the township, Blondie pointed out the massive Baragwanth Hospital on our left, "It's the only hospital in Soweto for a population of over eight hundred thousand!" We pulled over in a nearby taxi rank to view it. As we stood beside the kombi a sparkling new BMW roared in along side of us, it was Blondie's friend Alex Rantselli, who along with his brother Marc, were a chart-topping duo known as MarcAlex. Blondie introduced us, but to his surprise, we had already met during a phone interview. It was one more wonderful opportunity to connect face to face. Alex proudly showed off his new set of wheels and told me that he lived right there in Diepkloof. Years before my arrival, I had learned that Soweto wasn't, as most outsiders thought, one big slum. Certainly, the many photos taken amid the staggering poverty found in the informal settlements perpetuated that image.

As you enter Diepkloof, there are homes of various sizes, styles and upkeep. Except for the trash and the decaying body of a dead dog at the taxi rank, there was nothing terribly shocking. Alex shook his head in disgust and embarrassment saying, "We don't need to live like this." We exchanged good wishes and headed in deeper. Orlando East, Dube, Pimville, Protea, Zola, and more. The names fell from the lips of my hosts and sounded as familiar to me as neighborhoods in Philly. For several hours we slowly traversed the streets, winding through dirt road sections containing row after row of small, low, cinderblock constructed homes with corrugated rooftops; again, most well maintained, the result of proud homeowners.

Then, we'd pass into sections where children ran and played amidst trash, wastewater and those infamous shacks that had become synonymous with Soweto. This first visit was made more surreal by the site of large, beautiful homes, standing directly across the road from the squalor of informal settlements like Mshenguville. Of course, the fine homes stand surrounded by high walls and strong iron gates. Connie tells me that despite the violence, many upwardly mobile people were moving in to Soweto and not out. That surprised me because some friends who now live in Jo'burg had expressed real fear at venturing back in to Soweto where they had grown up. Paradox reigns supreme here.

As we rolled on, Blondie often made a point of stopping to talk to fans and to the children who ran along side the kombi; it was obvious they were happy to see one of their own back home in the township. We stopped at Nelson Mandela's home on Vilakazi Street, where a little over a year before, he returned from 27 years in prison. There wasn't a soul around except us. The garage was still painted in ANC colors. I remembered watching the paint job as it happened live on the news. Now, here I was standing in front of it. They took me to the spot where young Hector Pieterson was shot dead by the police on June 16, 1976 igniting the Soweto Uprising. It was a somber stop on our tour as my guides related their memories of the turmoil and tragedy of that day, and of the months that followed.

Blondie and Vusi pointed out a railway station where a week earlier commuters were attacked by machete wielding members of Inkatha, killing several people on the platform. On and on it went, details of a tragic history that was still being written in blood, courtesy of the escalating *black on black* violence, the favorite phrase of the government.

It was getting on toward noon and Blondie suggested we visit a small shebeen for a beer and a bite to eat. Normally, shebeens do their biggest business at night, but since it was Blondie, the proprietor welcomed us with open arms. All four of my hosts regaled me with shebeen stories of their wilder days; fights, police, women, politics, going out back to take a piss. A few beers, snacks and a classic male bullshit session almost made me forget where I was…almost. After our break, we were off again, this time to Blondie's childhood home in the section called Tladi. The narrow dirt street was devoid of any vehicular traffic expect for our kombi; the only other movement was a young, barefoot schoolgirl headed for home while playfully dragging a long stick in the dirt behind her. Blondie's home, now occupied by his sister, looked like so many others surrounding it. One story, corrugated tin roof, cinderblock walls, a tiny, barren front yard situated behind a small wooden fence. The home consisted of 4 rooms; a small living room, a galley kitchen, and two equally sized, small bedrooms.

The home tour didn't take long. We stepped out of the backdoor and in to the rear yard which contained another cinderblock structure. This tiny outbuilding was home to a young couple who couldn't afford to live anywhere else, and who didn't want to end up in one of the informal settlements. Blondie introduced me and insisted that I take their photo to illustrate how people were forced to live. I couldn't bring myself to exploit them as they sat staring, emotionless on their cot. I'd never make a successful photo-journalist. While I admire those in the trade, I found it nearly impossible to take such photos.

Off to our right, Blondie noticed that his neighbors and their aged father were sitting in their rear yard. We went over to say hello. Blondie introduced me to the younger members of the family and then leaned over to speak to this very frail veteran of a million hard days. He spoke in Sotho and explained to the old man who I was. He looked up at me from his chair with weak half opened eyes, gingerly stood up with the help of his cane, removed his cap, lowered his head in a subservient posture and extended his hand. It was all I could do to keep from bursting into tears. Apartheid had totally stripped this man of his dignity and I felt nothing but guilt because of it. I lowered my head in an effort to make eye contact and asked Blondie to tell him how truly honored I was to meet him. That small gesture brought a smile to his wrinkled face, but did little to lessen my guilt.

It was early evening when we made our final stop at the home of an old acquaintance of my host. The kombi pulled up to a cracker box of a home, literally two rooms, perhaps 400 square feet. Like others I had seen, it was spotless outside and inside. Apartheid hadn't stripped this homeowner of her dignity. We entered the small front room containing a few pieces of furniture. The surreal nature of this place strikes, for on the modest wall hung a framed gold LP. From out of the back room comes a short, stout smiling woman who embraces Blondie. "Mama" he smiles, not his biological mother, just a respectful "Mama".

He introduces me and tells me that her daughter was awarded the gold LP for her latest recording, a record that was huge in South Africa at the moment. Mama, beams with pride as she takes me over to view it up close. In an effort to once again impress upon me how life in Soweto is lived, he says "Mama, tell James how many people live in this house." She paused for a moment, counting to herself before saying "Eleven", explaining that she doesn't want any of her family or extended family "living in those filthy settlements, so they live here." Blondie and Mama insist that I take a picture of the gold LP. Since she was beaming with pride, I agree and feel that same sense of guilt creep back in to my soul. Before heading out, Blondie asks to buy some sorghum beer, which I had heard about, and something called mogodu, of which I had no idea. She went back in to the kitchen and came out with two large, white plastic jugs, they looked to be gallon size. Blondie paid and we were off.

Back in the kombi, the sorghum beer is opened and passed to the guest of honor…me! It's milky white with a flavor I have no ability to describe. Not horrible, but unlike anything I've ever tasted before. I drink and pass it on. They then open the mogodu and pull out small, strips of meat and pass it to me. I take some; pop it in my mouth, chewed on the slightly tuff meat and swallow; a sip of beer and I go back for more. MK asks while I am in mid-chew, "So, you eat tripe at home?" With a mouthful of tripe I force a smile, an agreeable nod, swallow, and quickly ask for the beer! It was dark by the time we arrived back at Blondie's office. We entered the lobby and were walking toward the stairwell when Blondie spotted an elderly gentleman sweeping the lobby floors. Blondie called to him, "Heita (*a township hello*), Baba (*father*), here's my friend from America I told you about." The man, along with his broom approached me, shook my hand vigorously and said in a chillingly serious voice "Please, tell the world what they are doing to us here in South Africa." The impact of his request shook me and I remember saying only "I will Baba." Blondie noticed my reaction to this exchange, and from the look on his face I could tell that he was pleased. He knew he was succeeding in his mission to change my life with this visit.

A Scrap of Humor

Alarm clock? Who needs one of those? You had to have been asleep for it to be of any use. The goal of my friends was to make certain that I experienced as much of South Africa as possible. To accomplish that goal meant surviving on almost no sleep, or perhaps a precious hour or two. The reason for my sleep deprivation was easy to diagnose, sensory overload. The faces, voices, music, noise, and even smells would repeat over and over during the quiet hours of the night. After the telephone call with Charlottie at 3 a.m., with the Special Branch listening in, the replay of the day's events would be kicked in to overdrive until dawn.On this particular sunny morning Sipho and I are off to visit a not so historic sight, a Soweto scrap yard. Living within a few hours of Washington D.C., my wife and I knew a little bit about playing the role of tour guide for friends and family visiting from out of state. We'd take the train down to the nation's capital and escort our guests to the various landmark attractions in D.C. *Must See* stops included the Capital building, the White House, the high reaching Washington Monument, and the many incarnations of the Smithsonian Institute. As a tour guide, never in my wildest dreams would I think that a scrap yard would be a worthwhile destination, but this is South Africa, and even a taste of what on the surface seems to be non-political, non-struggle related real life can fool you. Sipho needed a replacement petrol line for his ailing fire engine red Ford. The cracked windscreen was workable, you could still see traffic, stop signs and thankfully pedestrians; but those petrol fumes were a major headache in every sense of the word.

When we went anywhere we'd have to ride with the windows rolled all the way down, or risk not surviving the journey. Off we go to Soweto, fumes and all. Like any major city, the township was bustling with morning rush-hour traffic both mobile and pedestrian. We zigzagged around taxis picking up commuters, avoided an endless number of police vehicles, people walking, running or staggering along the streets, and managed to dodge lorry drivers who seemed to declare that safe driving was not their forte. Despite its overuse to describe a personal experience, *surreal* remains the word of words to explain what it was like to again find myself traveling through Soweto. I could see in my mind the police raids, the toyi-toying protesters, and mass funerals that filled these streets on the TV news back home. Trust me, surreal works very well. With a sharp swerve to the right and dust flying in our wake, we arrived at our destination and my imaginings end.

There is one universal truth regarding scrap or junkyards; they look the same the world over. Dirt parking area, scrap cars stacked on top of one another, wheel covers adorning the walls both inside and out of a shabby office, and terror inducing dogs that want nothing more than to kill you, or at least bite a big chunk out of some important body part. We head toward one of the endless rows of scrap autos where Sipho tells the attendant the specific part he's interested in obtaining. They chat a bit in Xhosa and Sipho suggests that I go and wait in the office while the two of them go off scrap hunting.

Inside the office I was surprised to see that a short, white, beer-bellied Afrikaner is headman. He doesn't seem to notice me as he was assisting a white customer. Now, I'm really confused. What the hell is a white guy doing buying parts from another white guy in a Soweto scrap yard? They are chatting away in Afrikaans when Mr. Headman grabs a small microphone and calmly announces in English, "I need a Stripper." Not being in the scrap business myself, I still figured out that a *Stripper* is someone capable of stripping desired parts off of the scrap cars, and this guy needed one, and now. They continue talking for a few minutes more. By their demeanor, it seemed to just be shit talk, when he again picked up his little mic and repeated his request for a Stripper…this time with a bit more force, thus causing a bit more blood to rush in to his chubby cheeks.

A few more minutes go by, and still, no Stripper appears to answer his call. All this time the two guys paid zero notice of me. While the customer was chatting away, I could see the distracted headman looking around for the Stripper, not really listening at all. Then, he let out an audible sigh, snatched the mic, stretching every inch of kink out of the cord and screams in full voice, "I NEED A STRIPPER!!!" The distorted, feedback-inducing outburst was so loud I thought I had suffered permanent hearing loss. It was all I could do to keep from laughing as he struggled several times to slam the mic back in its cradle. His face was crimson red and his breathing labored. This guy looked a few short beats from a heart attack.

The customer actually recoiled away from the counter after the explosion, perhaps reconsidering his choice of scrap yards. The office fell totally silent, expect for the heavy breathing of the pre-coronary headman. Then, from within the storeroom behind him, there came a slight noise; the doorknob turned and out stepped the dearly sought after Stripper. Dressed in dark blue work coveralls, he seemed to be moving in slow motion as if nothing in the world could hurry him. There is a saying in comedy, "timing is everything". How true, for just as the agonizingly slow moving Stripper made his way up to the boiling hot headman, Sipho came in and stood beside me. This causes the Headman to finally look in my direction. Totally flustered by the ordeal, and obviously thinking that since I was white I must be one of his own kind, he shakes his head in disgust and grunts "Ag, THESE people hey?" I smiled broadly and said with great delight as I pointed to Sipho, "I wouldn't know. I'm with HIM," pointing to Sipho. It felt good to have a bit of a laugh amid the scrap, even if I was laughing on the inside.

Hotel Apartheid

From the first day of my arrival at the Protea Gardens Hotel in Berea, it was obvious that my stay wouldn't be a particularly pleasant one. Those hateful looks cast at Sipho when he dropped me off and the rather icy reception from Reception drove that point home. "Forgetting" to give me time sensitive phone messages, not taking messages at all or never mentioning that someone had stopped by to see me were all part of the stellar service. I'm certain that I pissed off the bitch at reception when I would greet my friends with a big hug and we'd talk and laugh. She was not thrilled having these *blacks* sitting in *their* lobby. I would always have a good chuckled when, in my limited free time, I would leave to walk the few blocks up to Hillbrow. My racist, and yet well-meaning reception clerk would say things like "don't carry your camera or recorder…*they* will take it right from you!" The extra inflection on *they* was quite humorous. Who could she possibly be talking about? It reminded me of the warnings of my youth when the *they* in question were the same color as the *they* she mentioned. All of her helpful advice would carry the disclaimer "I'm only trying to warn you." I'd simply smile and say "I'll be fine" and she would glare red-faced and angry.

One of the primary streets through Hillbrow is Pretoria Street. I'd walk it for blocks past derelict apartment buildings, boarded up shops and a variety of shops that still held their own against the oncoming blight. It was sad to know that at the dawning of a new South Africa, this once iconic section of the city was near death. Maybe that's as it should be. There were bookstores, clothing shops, and small walk-in and open to the street eateries, as well as a wild collection of street vendors rivaling any big city in the world. A great little record shop afforded me the opportunity to buy some South African CDs that even my record company contacts didn't have. I also picked up a brand new copy of "Learn Zulu" and the follow-up "Learn MORE Zulu". Until I had these in my possession, I was studying from the photocopied version of "Learn Zulu" sent to me by the professor of African Studies at Yale.

Hillbrow was also the home of the *Twilight Children*, homeless bands of children who lived life rough on the streets. *Twilight Children* makes it sound romantic doesn't it? Pathetically tragic is more accurate. During one of my walks along Pretoria Street I stopped at open-air burger shop to spend the few Rand that I had on me. Once served, I took my burger and fries to a table off to the side. After an initial bite of my burger, I leaned over to place my camera and recorder on the floor next to me. When I sat up, there in the chair opposite me was a young boy, no more than ten, who appeared out of nowhere. Shoeless and wearing a tattered sweater, he spoke only with his eyes.

He looked down at my fries and then up at me. My newfound lunch companion didn't need to say a word, I understood completely. I slid the fries over to him and gave him half of my burger. We ate in silence. When he finished, he quietly slid from the chair and disappeared in the crowded street. Heading back down toward my hotel, I kept wondering, could the receptionist have meant this small boy? Is he the *they?* She seemed to hate me for bringing blacks in to the hotel, so why all the advice and warnings? As annoying as these lapses of caring for my welfare were, I put it down to ignorance and fear, all part of the apartheid mentality. I was willing to give her the benefit of the doubt, until the day she pushed me too far, to paraphrase P.W. Botha.

My friend and isiZulu teacher back in Philadelphia, Sibongile Sithole, was in South Africa visiting her family. Sipho was going to bring Sibongile, her daughter Ayanda, as well as Sibongile's sister to the hotel to see me, sometime around 5:00 p.m. I had a full day planned but made certain to be back by 4:00. I told the reception clerk, yes *that* reception clerk, that I was expecting friends and to ring up to my room when they arrived. While waiting in my room, I used the time to review some taped interviews. Marks Mankwane started playing guitar at the age of twelve. By the mid nineteen sixties, he became one of the founding members of the legendary session band the Makgona Tsohle Band. Roughly translated, it means *(the band that can do anything)*. It was during this period that the band teamed with *groaner* vocalist Simon "Mahlathini" Nkabinde, and the township music known as *mbaqanga* was born.

Once again, our meeting was made that much more familiar and relaxed as a result of our having spoken many times on the phone. For such a vibrant guitarist, I was surprised by the soft-spoken nature of the man as we sat in the band's rehearsal studio in Johannesburg. When asked to describe how he and the band felt about their newfound popularity throughout Europe and now the United Sates, Marks grinned and exclaimed,

"This has been a great year for all of us. We are so happy to have been able to introduce our music, our *mbaqanga* music to America."

Then, with a shake of his head he chuckled to himself continuing, "Fifteen to twenty years back I never thought our music can really reach as far as America!"

When I asked him about the apparent lack of interest in *mbaqanga* style guitar playing among some young musicians Marks expressed disappointment. "To be honest, when I started this kind of guitar style I play, lots of young players were very interested. Then, all of a sudden they start to copy lots of great stars from the west! They don't want to create their own music, from their own culture, and yet South Africa is full of great talent."

Still, because of the overseas success he and the band were enjoying he had hopes that things would change. "It's funny, even though some want to play like Jimi Hendrix or George Benson, they see us touring overseas and ask me, "*how is it you are so popular overseas when it isn't even their culture?*" I tell them, it is because we stuck to our roots and our own culture. I'm happy to say that more of these young people are now turning back to their culture and play original South African music."

In the years to follow, Marks and I would meet many times as the group performed in Philadelphia. With each visit, appreciative crowds grew bigger and bigger.

A quick check of the time…it was almost 6:00 p.m., and no Sipho. Normally, I would be a bit concerned, but over the years I had learned that to South Africans, *time* is simply a concept and not a hard, fast reality. Sipho was late coming to the airport, but he did come. Sipho himself told me of the many times he'd wait at home for a service person to come, only to have them show up extremely late, or not at all. Back home in the states, when South Africans were invited to our home for parties they were always the last to arrive. The fact that there was still no sign of Sipho wasn't a worry, back to my tape recorder I go. During those months and years of trying to get the program on the air, I would occasionally allow myself a brief stint of self-pity, lamenting that perhaps this just wasn't meant to be. As it turned out, those months and years afforded me time for research and learning, all of which paid dividends when it came to finally meeting the artists I had come to admire. I knew their histories and their music, and that created an instant connection. Such was the case with the man known by many in South Africa as Bra Ray.

Already a guitar and composing legend as a result of his work with the band Stimela, Chikapa Ray Phiri rose to worldwide fame as arranger, guitarist and co-writer on Paul Simon's *Graceland* CD and tour. Ray's thin build masks a hearty handshake and an ear-to-ear smile. To look at him, you'd think him frail. To see him dance and move on stage, he seems to have an endless supply of energy. He'd tell you it comes from the music. From the earliest days of the radio program, Ray and Stimela captured the attention of my listeners. One track in particular, *Whispers in the Deep* was guaranteed to generate calls every time I played it, all asking where it could be purchased. Noticeably political, I asked Ray what lead him to be so anti-government on record. "I got annoyed at people for mistaken my songs for love songs. I just wanted to call a spade a spade. No matter what, I have come out in the open. It's one particular track that took a lot out of me, personally". I knew that Ray, along with many other South African musicians had been invited to meet Nelson Mandela shortly after his release. "We were honored to have been invited, but I admit I was very nervous about meeting the man" Ray explained. "When we got there, and he came up to me I started to introduce myself and he stopped me and said "ah, come on now Ray, I KNOW who you are." Ray grinned as he recalled that day. When asked to describe his experience with Paul Simon's *Graceland* tour Ray said, "I knew that when I was out there, I was there trying to expose the world to South African music, and I was hoping that by the people hearing this great music, it would open doors for other South African musicians, so that their music could be heard".

Ray chuckled for a moment and said "it's funny, Paul is always asking me to stop dancing so much, he says that it's distracting, but I'm gonna keep right on dancing". Click, cassette player off.

Shit! 7:00 p.m., now I'm starting to worry. Are they coming or not? Did Sipho not hook up with Sibongile? I couldn't call him, he had no home phone, and cell phones were a rich man's pleasure in South Africa. While waiting, I switched on the TV set, up popped a full screen shot of a South African Police Services badge and the words *Ingalo Lomthetho* (Arm of the Law). This program was unlike anything I could ever have imagined. Speaking in Zulu, the unseen announcer would describe where and when various bodies were found. As he spoke, a close-up of a lifeless face was put on the screen. Some of the bodies had been severely marred by the violence that brought them to a starring role in this sick display. In between each of the faces of death, the big SAPS badge would slam on to the screen. The level of political violence in the townships around Johannesburg had reached the point where dozens of people were being killed everyday and their bodies dumped, or simply left where they fell. *Ingalo Lomthetho* was the SAPS quick fix to help identify the victims. When the morbid prime-time half hour had come to an end, I accepted the fact that Sipho wasn't coming. Hey, this is South Africa go with it. The only concern I had was what to do with my free evening.

Do I dare step out in to the night with or without my camera and recorder? I was mulling over my options when there came a knock on my door. It was a very angry Sipho. "James, where have you been?" He snapped. Before I could answer he continued, "We've been waiting for you downstairs since 5:15, Sibongile and her sister had to leave, so they finally took a taxi home at 7!" In utter disbelief I replied, "I've been here in my room since 4…waiting for you." Sipho looked confused. "But I had that woman at the desk call your room three or four times; she said you weren't answering and that she hadn't seen you return." The bitch had gone too far this time. Sipho went on to tell me that after Sibongile and her sister departed, he headed for the lifts and was told that him he couldn't go up because he wasn't a guest, thankfully he ignored her.

Once we realized that she had intentionally screwed our plans, I charged down to the desk to confront her. With a face filled with a false expression of concern, she offered a weak apology, one that seemed to also contain a sinister smile of delight."I must have dialed the wrong room" was her only reply to my raving. As Sipho and I headed out the door to visit a few clubs, I asked him a question I had asked many times before, and would ask several times to come, "Why haven't black people killed these fucking racists?" His answer showed a greater degree of rational thinking than I was capable of at the time, "We want equality and peace in South Africa, not a bloodbath." After this episode, I became so suspicious of the unreceptive receptionist that I removed my Travelers Checks and passport from my hotel lock box and hid them in my room.

Jo'burg by Night

For many years during the research and learning phase of my South
African experience, I had read about this club called Kippie's. From all
accounts, it was *the* jazz club in Johannesburg. Named after legendary
jazz composer and musician Kippie Moeketsi, it was the favorite
gathering spot for musicians and the serious jazz fan. Before I ever
arrived in Jo'burg I was afraid I'd never get to see it, due to the fact it
was always on the verge of going belly-up. Located in the Newtown
section of Johannesburg, a somewhat seedy part of the city, Kippie's,
along with its much larger neighbor the Market Theatre was
transforming the area in to the city's cultural center.

Before we headed to Kippie's Sipho insisted on taking me on a tour of
some of the cities other clubs, clubs where, as Sipho put it, "the rich
white kids go." Okay, I thought, after all, the scrap yard turned out to
be a load of laughs. What the hell is this then? These clubs were so
much like clubs in the states. It was as though I had never left
Philadelphia. Classic rock music blasting from semi-talented cover
bands, yuppie guys and girls posturing for one another as they spilled
their light beers; and lots of confused looks directed at Sipho,
seemingly the only black person in the place. Club after club, it usually
took all of a few minutes before I leaned over to Sipho and said in no
uncertain terms, "get me out of here!" Sipho wanted me to see the
"rich white kids" clubs; I saw them, now I want to go to Kippie's.

We got there around 10:00 pm, maybe later, just as things were starting to kick in. Boasting a seating capacity of maybe eighty, Kippie's was crowded; smoke filled and dark; in a word, exhilarating. Walking in with Sipho was like arriving with a celebrity, he knew practically everyone, and if he didn't, practically everyone knew him. Despite the fact that the place was packed to the rafters, we were ushered to a table; Sipho had some clout! On stage just to the right of the bar was a small impromptu group comprised of some of the country's hottest young musicians. Piano, guitar, bass and drums; these guys weren't a working band, just friends jamming, but WHAT jamming! It was jazz with a well-defined South African groove. Throughout the course of the evening various friends and acquaintances of Sipho's joined us at our tiny table; many of them musicians in groups with recording contracts, some without. Since the majority of them had never performed outside of South Africa they were keen on hearing my views regarding their music and how it might be received in the states.

There was lively political discussion to be sure, but the focus of most conversations was music. New approaches to producing, getting screwed by record labels, trying to crack the international market, staying true to the music. Factor in the crowd, smoke, beers and a kickass band providing the soundtrack; Kippie's exceeded all of my expectations. I have no recollection of what time it was when we left, but I do remember that it wasn't too long after I returned to my hotel room that Charlottie called at 3:00 am. After having dealt with *the bitch,* this turned out to be a good night.

Another evening of extraordinary live music unfolded before Sipho and I at The Cotton Pub, a funky downstairs bar located in the heart of Hillbrow. Just getting there provided me a glimpse at a unique urban culture. Perhaps this takes place in other major cities, but I had never seen men and boys *hold* a parking space in return for cash. As we drove around Hillbrow in search of a parking space near the club, a man or young boy would leap out in front of the car, whistle and point to a vacant spot. If you wanted it, you acknowledged him, parked the car and paid him. From what Sipho told me, the price could vary depending on the proximity to a well-known club, or you could simply negotiate the price. One thing you did not want to do was piss off the holder by not paying. You could very well return to your vehicle and find mysterious scratches and dents that weren't there earlier. After passing a few available spots that were not to Sipho's liking, we were flagged down by a holder offering a great space within walking distance of the Cotton Pub. We took it.

While Sipho paid the extortionist his fee, I was being accosted by a very drunk, very loud man repeatedly asking, "Unemali?" (*Do you have money?*). One bit of Zulu I learned quite well was my reply "Cha! Anginemali!" (*No! I have no money*). The man would not relent and the exchange went back and forth a few times. Sipho drew up near me to make certain I was okay, but he soon realized that my limited; or should I say, very limited Zulu had successfully gotten the message across.

Never having been what you would call a regular club patron in the states, that is to say I almost never went to clubs; I was surprised by our reception as we entered the Cotton Pub, we were vigorously searched. Then, I remembered where I was, South Africa, Johannesburg, Hillbrow. It all made sense. Cleared to get in, we headed down the stairs to the club and to greetings from Sipho's many friends. Tonight on stage, Loading Zone, the youthful and impressively tight house band.

All of these guys were in their early 20s and played like they were veterans of years of touring and recording. From original contemporary jazz inspired numbers to covers of Al Jarreau and George Benson, Loading Zone drew a young, hip, multi-ethnic crowd who knew these guys were something special, destined for greater success. Just as it had happened at Kippie's, we were ushered to an empty table, although there didn't seem to be one upon our arrival. Sipho's magic strikes again! I ordered beers for the two of us and was served a Castle, one of the most popular beers in South Africa. We drank our beers, listened to the band and chatted with the various friends who stopped by the table. Back in the states my beer of choice was strong English Ale, so for me, Castle was like drinking water, and I drank it down as such. Sipho asked "how do you like our South African beer?" I explained that my taste preference leaned toward something stronger. He suggested that for my second beer, I switch to Lion, a stronger beer.

The band took a break and we were joined at our table by the guitarist Jimmy Dludlu, who happened to be Sipho's nephew, and the percussionist John Hassan. While the four of us talked about music, politics and my impressions of South Africa, I drank down the Lion, just as I had done the Castle. Sipho explained to them that I thought South African beers were weak; all three suggested that I go for the strongest beer available, Black Label. "Black Label?" I asked. "Are we talking about the same Black Label beer? Red can, with black label in the middle, *that* Black Label?"

The answer was "Yes…do you know it?" Feeling a bit cocky, thanks to a slight *light beer* buzz, I said "I used to drink Black Label in high school, bring it on." My third beer was delivered and all three of my tablemates watched and waited for my review. Compared to the ales I was used to drinking, even Black Label was weak, however, it did outdo the Castle and Lion for taste. I chose to sing it praises and thanked my friends for their suggestion.

Loading Zone retook the stage and we were treated to another fabulous set. As their loyal fans knew, the band would go on to much greater success, playing with South African stars such as Miriam Makeba, Brenda Fassie, Chicco, Stimela, as well as African super-star Papa Wemba. In later years Jimmy Dludlu would go on to become a world-renown jazz guitarist, while John Hassan would become one of the most sought after percussionists in South Africa.

Jiggs

"These fucking Boers are shitting in their fucking pants man." Jiggs is a writer; a highly respected writer in South Africa. Naturally he has a way with words, especially one word, *fuck*. Jiggs loves this word. I'd like to say that he sprinkles it through conversations, using it for impact only, but that would be an understatement. Colin "Jiggs" Smuts, classified as *colored* by the color conscience apartheid machine is an anti-apartheid, cultural activist and very active in his branch of the ANC. Colin also happens to be the Director of The Open School, a cultural/educational program where children from the townships are encouraged to express themselves with confidence about their environment and their aspirations through dance, art, drama and music. The Security Branch (SBs) calls the school "a breeding ground for the ANC."

Like many of my connections in South Africa, I came to know Colin through phone conversations. The Open School had published a remarkable book called *Two Dogs and Freedom*. Written by students ranging in ages from 8 to 17, the book consisted of short essays and art detailing their view of life in South Africa. Profound, moving, unsettling; this little book was as powerful as any of the music I had featured on my program. With Colin's help, I arranged to have several dozen copies sent to the U.S. where I placed them in bookstores around the Philadelphia area. They sold out within weeks.

As it happened, Blondie knew Colin very well. He had used artwork done by the students on two of his album covers; and on this day was shooting a video at the Open School for his latest *banned* release. They were including some of the younger students dancing on stage with Blondie and his group Amaqabane. This was the perfect opportunity to finally meet Colin face to face and to interview a few of his students. The school was located in downtown Johannesburg and occupied several floors of an old office building. We headed up to the theatre, a large open room with a small stage and modest lighting; that's where I first met Colin.

His long, straight black hair hung down just short of his shoulders and swept across his forehead. A dark beard almost hid from view his mischievous grin. Mischievous is the perfect word to describe Colin, and his alter ego Jiggs. To add character to this character, he was wearing a Che' Guevara T-shirt and I'll be dammed if the two didn't look alike! One of Colin's most endearing qualities as a writer is his ability to find humor in everyday dealings with the fools who created and implemented apartheid. I had learned from many that a sense of humor was an essential tool if you are to survive life under apartheid. Outgoing and funny as hell, it was easy to like Colin in an instant. I lost count of how many "fucks" passed his lips in our greeting, but his take on current events and what may come next had me in stitches

He took me through the school, proudly showing me the various classrooms where students from the townships would find a little peace through creativity. Funding was always an issue, and as you might expect, a good many "fucks" drove home the point of just how difficult it was to keep the place alive. I met his teenage son Themba, his name means *Hope*. Here was living proof that there was a soft side to this cynical, sarcastic guy. Even with all the "horrible shit going down" in South Africa he named his son Themba. He went on to tell me that over the years the Security Branch would raid the place on a regular basis looking for student troublemakers.

Colin introduced me to one such trouble-maker, now a staff member named Peter. Years earlier he was a student activist sought by the police. One day the SBs raided the school looking for Peter. As they were going floor to floor conducting their search, word reached the floor he was on. With no time to lose and the security branch heading down the hall toward them, Peter ran and locked himself in the Resource Center. The SBs demanded the key; Colin told them that another co-worker had taken it home. Thankfully, the silly sods believed the story and left the building. Quickly Colin and an assistant returned to the Resource Center, opened the door with a spare key and discovered that Peter was nowhere to be found. They suddenly realized that the key to the large office safe was missing. Peter had locked himself inside the safe with the key!

They shouted toward the safe, telling him it was okay to come out. After a brief pause, they heard a click, the door opened and out stepped Peter. However, their problems were far from over. Several SBs were now set up just outside, waiting. Since they were looking for a young man with a bushy Afro and goatee, it was time to transform Peter, and quickly. With the only razor they could find, old and not very sharp, they shaved Peter's goatee, and clothed him in what looked like an old man's suit taken from their drama department. As the staff departed for the day, among them walked a slow moving elderly man, out the door, past his predators, in to a taxi and was gone. Unfortunately, some weeks later, an *impimpi*, (informer) gave Peter up to the authorities. He was arrested, tortured and held in detention for over a year. I couldn't help wondered to myself, after all of this, how in the hell is Peter this friendly, outgoing person standing here before me?

Next up on my Open School agenda was a round of interviews with the students themselves. Colin seated me in a makeshift conference room and ushered in the students, one at a time. Like the students who contributed to the book, they ranged in age from 10 to 17. He explained to them beforehand who I was and what I was doing back in the states. I was both impressed and deeply saddened at how politically intelligent these children were.

10-year old Nomsa. "Here in South Africa we are struggling for one thing…freedom. In Soweto you cannot go at night. We don't know if Inkatha are there or not. The police are working with Inkatha and they are killing us."

17-year old Jabu. "I think people In the United States don't know the *real* thing of what is happening here in South Africa. They think that apartheid is over and I can tell them, apartheid is not over. This government is buying Inkatha to kill members ANC."

12-year old Elda. "I would like that every human being, be it black or white, every human being must have a job. In a new South Africa, it will be no apartheid."

17-year old Perseverance. "I think America, I don't think that they think we are suffering; maybe because they don't know the truth. They have not been given the truth. We are suffering very badly."

16-year old Sipho. "We wanted Nelson Mandela and all of the political prisoners to be taken out of prison, but that is not all. We want a new South Africa where by everyone will have a say in the running of the country."

15-year old Alfred. "Where I live in Soweto, last week these people of Inkatha were moving with the police. Many people told the police, this must stop…the violence must stop, but it has not stopped."

With each story I kept thinking, shouldn't a 10-year old girl be happily skipping rope with friends? Shouldn't a 13-year old boy know more about sport then how the police were arming members of Inkatha? These children knew about the talks between the ANC and the government. They knew who was behind the *third force* element inciting the current violence. They were well versed on key issues such as the need for jobs, public and social services, as well as revamping of the police services. I made a point of asking them about their art, music and other hobbies, that's when they were able to become children and I could hear the joy in their voices.

Nearly 20 years after our meeting, I can still hear their voices in my head and see their stern expressions as they detailed life in South Africa for this American visitor. I had often wondered what became of these children of the township. Colin recently told me he knows that some of them "have really turned out well", but since the school was closed he has lost touch with many of them. After I concluded my final interview, Colin invited me to join him and his wife for dinner, for what he described as, "The best fucking Indian food in the whole country." Who could resist such an eloquent invitation?

That evening, Colin picked me up and first took me to his home in Fluerhof where I met his wife, whose name I can no longer recall. Yes, they too lived in the same stylish black and colored suburb where Blondie lived, a stone's throw from Soweto. After a few tumblers of scotch or whiskey, I wasn't really sure which; I was treated to Colin's hilarious explanation of how blacks and coloreds had taken over Fluerhof. "When white motherfuckers realized if the blacks attacked their ass, they're coming right over that fucking field. So they got the fuck out." Every Colin story is told through contagious snorts of laughter. Where do you go in South Africa when you want "the best fucking Indian food in the whole country?" You go to the Indian neighborhood of course. Before dinner I was given the tour. As I marveled at some spectacular homes, Colin explained that "Indians do a whole lot better in South Africa. They're great business people." It was a remarkable evening.

Over dinner, Colin and his wife spoke of what it was like to grow up *colored* in South Africa. "At times you are not accepted by some in the black community" she explained "because they think you're getting preferential treatment." Colin continued, "While you are only slightly tolerated by the fucking white community, who *maybe* treat you somewhat better, depending on how light your fucking skin color may be." Once again I felt honored to be so trusted and accepted by people I had just met that same day. And to paraphrase Jiggs, it was the best fucking Indian food I've ever tasted.

Deep Soweto 10:00 p.m.

You don't have to possess a medical degree to know that consecutive nights without sleep can be detrimental to your health, especially your emotional and mental health. I was beginning to see signs of this in myself. For years I had been doing almost nothing in my personal life that didn't involve something to do with South Africa. Now, here I was, seeing it up close in a constant barrage of people, places and stories; exciting and depressing, sometimes all at once. My feeble brain has only so much room to take in and store data; overload was beginning to worry me. My emotional up and down visit was quickly making me the poster child for Mr. Manic 1991. I craved a day that was *close* to normal. This was to be that day. At least it started out that way.

Eleanor Campbell, one of the program's most steadfast supporters, worked as an executive for Gallo Music Group, the largest and oldest independent record label in South Africa. Tall, attractive and of Scottish decent, her dark red hair bore a streak of frosted color. From my earliest contact with Gallo, Eleanor made certain that I received not only new releases from bands like Stimela, Lucky Dube, Ladysmith Black Mambazo and Mahlathini, but also a wide variety of archived music, especially jazz from the forties and fifties. We met face to face for the first time at the braai that Blondie had in my honor. On this morning, it was nothing quite as elaborate, just breakfast with her boss Charles Kuhn, the CEO of Gallo.

I was sitting in the lobby ignoring *the bitch* at reception when they arrived at 8:00. Seems like everything in South Africa, at least during my visit, revolved around an 8 a.m. start! Charles looked to be in his early fifties, graying hair and very distinguished in a dark blue suit. Eleanor wore a beauty dark business suit as well, and carried a large bundle of LPs for me. It's funny, as I think of it now, they were the first *white* people to come to the hotel to collect me. I didn't think to check out the expression on *the bitch's* face.

Over breakfast Charles asked me the questions that were becoming standard fare. How? When? Why? Etc. I was flattered that the CEO of Gallo would give me his card and said "anytime you need something and can't get Eleanor, call me." When I asked him "why didn't Gallo and other labels jump on the success of Graceland, and rush South Africa's top groups to the US quickly?" He replied, "James, we blew it." His frankness impressed me, "There's no better way to put it. We sat on our collective asses, and we blew it." The remainder of my day was spent at Gallo, meeting staff, answering the same questions over and over. If I had a personal doctor in South Africa, I'm convinced he would have said, "That day was just what the doctor ordered, very relaxed and instructive."

My night would prove to be something altogether different. Sipho was taking me to meet and have dinner with his mother in deep Soweto. I don't know where or when I first heard the term, *deep Soweto,* but you don't need to be South African to understand its meaning. If confession is good for the soul, I admit to being a little apprehensive about the outing. Sure, I wanted to meet Sipho's mother, but the level of random political violence between Inkatha and ANC supporters was making everyone nervous about going in to Soweto, especially at night. Sipho's mother lived in a section called Protea, very near a notorious police station where countless numbers of students and suspected *terrorists* were regularly detained.

One such detainee was my friend Mzwakhe Mbuli. Mzwakhe was arrested for concealing a hand grenade in his home. He was stripped naked and held in solitary confinement for six months. Years later, when the Truth and Reconciliation Commission was hearing cases and granting amnesty to political criminals from both sides, Mzwakhe's arresting officer confessed to planting the grenade; big surprise there! After having seen the rising body count on the TV show *Ingalo Lomtetho*, I had to ask Sipho if he thought it was safe. His response was "James, if we are meant to die…so be it." At first, I wasn't sure if he was serious or just being dramatic, I settled on serious. That's the way life was being lived in this country. You could either get on with it or hide in fear. I climbed in to the passenger seat and we headed off toward whatever was meant to be.

It was already dark by the time we entered Soweto and headed in deeper toward Protea. Sipho was motoring along at a fair speed as we approached one of the few traffic lights in the township; it had gone red. To my surprise, Sipho gave the brakes a slight tap, took a quick look in both directions and motored through the red light. He explained, "You don't stop at robots in Soweto, that's where many car-jackings and Inkatha killings are taking place." Since there didn't seem to be any other traffic around I wasn't too concerned. As we drove past an informal settlement I was struck by the eerie sight of heavy coal smoke descending on the tiny shacks like a shroud. Surreal sensations were becoming commonplace. A minor spell of paranoia surfaced when we pulled in to a petro station where a small group of men were standing just outside the office area. In a stern voice Sipho said "James, stay in the car."

He went inside, and for a brief moment, I quickly became the focal point. Do they think I'm a policeman perhaps? Why else would this *umlungu* (white man) be here? Trying to show my sense of *cool and calm,* I rolled my window down and did my best impression of looking relaxed. In no time they went back to their conversation, offering occasional glances my way. Sipho was back in a flash and off we went. We cruised past the ominous Protea Police station, turned and pulled up to the home of his mother.

Like so many homes in Soweto, it was humble and very tidy, just a few rooms including a small living room with a couple of chairs and a portable TV. The adjoining dining area contained a rectangular table covered in a delicate lace tablecloth. Joining us for dinner was Sipho's cousin, and her husband. His mother greeted me as an honored guest. She was a heavy woman with a broad toothless smile, tightly cut gray hair and the kind of large eyeglasses older people tend to favor. Sipho had told her all about me and she was genuinely happy to meet me. I endeavored to use my poor command of isiZulu to thank her for her kind invitation. She nodded and accepted my attempt with a happy grin.

She asked me a question in Xhosa, her native language that I barely understood, but knew it had something to do with speaking Zulu. Sipho translated, "My mother wants to know why you choose to speak Zulu and not Xhosa?" Since she could understand some English, I choose to respond in my native language. "Mama, Xhosa has so many click sounds I knew I could never master it, so I chose Zulu, which I can speak a little." Despite my answer, she still felt that I should study Xhosa. Here again, another example of the divide that existed between Xhosa and Zulu people.

Our dinner was a deliciously hearty stew of beef and vegetables with fresh baked crusty bread. The three men sat around the table in the dining area, while Sipho's mother and cousin sat on kitchen chairs in the living room. As men, we were of course served first and waited on by the younger of the two women. The women watched TV while they ate; the men discussed the politics of the day, wondered about the future and answered my many questions about life in Soweto. After dinner, it was TV time for all of us.

We settled in and watched a late News cast, more politics, more violence, and more discussion. It was well after 10:00 p.m. when Sipho and I got ready for the return, me to Johannesburg and Sipho to Vosloorus. I hugged his mother and told her how honored I was to be invited and to have enjoyed such a delicious meal. I also said that I would endeavor to learn Xhosa as well. She expressed her pleasure at having met her son's American brother and invited me back when I returned to South Africa.

We made our way through the darkened streets of Protea heading toward the primary road that would take us out of Soweto. I was providing Sipho with my assessment of the evening when our faces were illuminated by the high beams of an oncoming sedan. It was straight ahead of us and in our lane. Sipho quickly reduced his speed.

As the sedan drew even closer, I heard him mutter "uh-oh." I thought to myself, "Shit. We really ARE going to be killed tonight." Surprised at the sense of calmness that I felt, I was resigned to the fate that Charlottie had foreseen. We were almost at a crawl when the oncoming sedan slowly veered to the left so it could pass on my side. Sipho warned, "Don't look at them…look straight ahead." They passed within inches of us, almost stopping. I looked straight ahead as instructed but could tell that the vehicle was a white four-door sedan, nothing more. Suddenly, they accelerated and were gone in an instant. We both drew a deep breath and Sipho wondered if they were police, *tsotsi*s (gangsters) or Inkatha. The remainder of our journey home was without incident, filled only with thoughts of what could have happened in the very violent world that was Soweto 1991.

Zulu Sunday

Talks About Talks- The spin machinery from the various political parties had to say *something* positive. It had been over eighteen months since Mandela's release, and people needed to feel that some kind of progress toward some kind of democratic process was being made. The buzz that *Talks About Talks* were going to take place was the best they could come up with. Meanwhile, Inkatha, the ANC and the Third Force element continued their bloody warfare. This was the environment in which my first week in South Africa came to an end. Thanks to the iconic presence of Nelson Mandela and the news of *Talks,* South Africa remained a worthy media topic. As a result, Johnny Clegg and his band Savuka were able to ride a tidal wave of U.S. media attention.

Johnny had already cracked the international music scene during the 1980s with his first band Juluka. Now, thanks to *Mandela Mania*, they were appearing on programs such as the Tonight Show, Saturday Night Live and on numerous television specials. Johnny's unique musical melding of Zulu and English cultures proved to be quite accessible to the U.S. audience, and his career was booming. As stated earlier in these pages, Johnny was one of my most important advisors. His life experience and knowledge were resources I drew on repeatedly. He knew that if a white man, especially a white American wished to tell a South African story, it would require credibility that was irreproachable.

We had met a few times while he was touring in Philadelphia and we spoke regularly on the phone. When Johnny learned that I would be coming to South Africa he was eager to immerse me in Zulu culture as deeply as time would allow. His hope was that I would accompany him to KwaZulu Natal to attend the wedding of a friend. While I would have loved the experience, I had to decline; I would only be in Johannesburg for fifteen days.

It was toward the end of my first week in Jo'burg when I phoned him. He asked, "Do you have any plans for Sunday?" "None at the moment" I replied. "Great. Have you been to the hostels yet?" He was referring to the large workers hostels that house thousands of migrant workers, many of them from the rural Zulu territory, the majority being members of Inkatha. I told him that Blondie had driven me up to a few of the larger hostels in Soweto, but we didn't dare go in due to the ANC colors that adorned Blondie's kombi. "Great" said Johnny, "I want to take you to where my guys are."

Johnny was talking about the hostel that served as his *school* during the days of his youth, the place where he was surrounded by the music, dance and culture of the Zulu people. That place was the George Goch Hostel.

To Americans, the name means nothing, but to South Africans living in and around Johannesburg in 1991, and to me, now totally consumed with all things South African, the George Goch Hostel was home to state sponsored killers. The violence between Inkatha and ANC supporters was widespread by this time and the George Goch Hostel was reportedly Inkatha headquarters in Johannesburg. Its residents were suspected of committing several brutal murders, including a recent bloody slaughter of 13 mourners at a night vigil in the nearby township of Alexandria. On more than one occasion, police conducted raids on the hostel, but to the surprise of no-one, never seemed to find weapons or make a single arrest.

Johnny was to arrive at my hotel around 11:00 a.m. that Sunday morning, the first time that my day didn't start at 8! This gave me a bit of time for an early morning walk up to Hillbrow to see the sights. Not that I was looking for it, but where was the danger? I returned to the hotel around 10:30 and sat outside the entrance on a nearby bench. Johnny pulled up in his kombi and came over to greet me. After phone conversations and backstage meetings in Philadelphia, it was wonderful to see him on his home-turf. We climbed in and headed off. First, we took a quick tour of Johannesburg from his perspective. Like Blondie and Sipho before him, Johnny pointed out sights historic and tragic, and lamented the rapid decline of Hillbrow and areas like it.

Our conversation was relaxed and intimate. In an interview for a TV special earlier in the year, Johnny spoke of how he was drawn to Zulu culture stating, "They knew something I could never know." We talked about that interview on the phone shortly after it aired and I mentioned it again during our ride to George Goch Hostel. I told him about the parting from my wife, the long hours lost in thought on the journey to South Africa and the endless stream of visions that were keeping me awake every night. Johnny said he knew that I was "seeking something" and understood the incomplete feeling all to well because as he put it "I've been there." Of course the topic of politics and recent events became part of our conversation. Johnny told me that he was feeling pressure from members of both the ANC and rival Inkatha to choose a side; and to state it publicly. He often spoke of and sang about Mandela, a democratic South Africa and voting rights for all; therefore, he must be very pro-ANC.

Yet, he had embraced Zulu culture so vigorously that the Zulu based Inkatha believed he must stand with them. Certainly, he embraced Zulu culture, but he steadfastly refused to show support for Inkatha, constantly condemning the violence that its members perpetrated. He told both parties that his politics were his own and were not for sale.

Johnny sighed and told me again how very sad he was to know that "some of my guys were probably behind these murders." We had arrived at George Goch Hostel. The hostel compound was comprised of several multi-floor, unimpressive brick buildings with a large parking area in the rear. It had the appearance of a long neglected, inner-city apartment complex.

This being Sunday, all of the workers were enjoying a day off and were relaxing in the parking area. As we rolled through the lot shouts of "*Juluka*" were directed toward Johnny. Clearly these people knew and respected this "white Zulu" as he had come to be called in the press. Perhaps it was my imagination, but the mood seemed to be anything but jovial. Yes, music was playing, grills were in use, and gallons of home brewed beer were being consumed, but there was a tangible uneasiness in the air. We stopped to chat a few times with men he knew, but he expressed sadness because he said, "the whole feeling here is now very different, the violence had changed everything." He wanted to move on, and so we did. We pulled out of the compound and headed to the nearby warehouse district where Johnny was exposed to various styles of Zulu dance.

He parked the kombi on an empty street, flanked on both sides by long, windowless warehouses. Another sigh of disappointment was uttered as Johnny explained, "this place used to be packed with people on Sundays, now nobody comes because of the violence."

We walked a short distance up to an intersection where two different Zulu dance groups were practicing on opposite sides of the street. We were the only two spectators in sight. One group consisted of seven men; all but one squatting in a circle on the sidewalk. The leader, with whistle in his mouth, would hover over the group, blow the whistle and enthusiastically point to an individual. The chosen dancer-warrior leapt to his feet and entered the circle. Music was provided by a large bass drum and a pounding beat; the only accompaniment was the sound of the men clapping in unison to the beat. As if in a trance, the warrior fought an enemy only he could see. Stabbing out against his foe; kicking his legs high in to the air and stamping the ground delivering a mighty blow. His dance would end by falling to the ground as if struck down in battle and the leader would then choose another warrior.

The second group of men followed a different form of dance. The six man troupe stood together in a line and moved in unison; again, fighting enemies only they could see and dying the same death together. Their accompaniment wasn't a drum, but was provided by a few non-dancing members who hummed a deep, penetrating hum and clapped in unison to the melody they hummed. Why I carried my camera and tape recorder I don't know, because I couldn't bring myself to use them. I was afraid of breaking the spell that was being cast. I truly understood what Johnny meant, and he was right; these guys know something I could never know, and I envied them, then and now.

A misty rain fell upon the warriors as we drove off toward our next destination, Mai Mai Bazaar; the oldest market in Johannesburg. Originally built in the 1940s as stables for the refuse collection horses, the compound of over 175 units now housed traditional healers, makers of traditional clothing, shoes and weapons. Like George Goch Hostel, Mai Mai was at the epicenter of Zulu culture in Johannesburg. We came to a stop at a red light a few blocks from Mai Mai, where off to our right I saw two men and a woman standing on the corner. One of the men was violently slapping the woman, who wept and recoiled only to be pulled back and slapped again and again. As disturbing as this violence was to witness, even more disturbing was the reaction of the second man. He stood casually by, watching as if it were entertainment. For a moment he looked over toward Johnny and me, then back to the sobbing woman. The light went green, Johnny stepped on the gas saying, "This is my biggest problem with Zulu culture, their treatment of women, but you cannot intervene."

The disturbing vision of the abuse we had witnessed remained with me as we parked the kombi outside of Mai Mai and entered through its high iron gates. My senses were overtaken by a multitude of sights, sounds and smells. The former stables are low brick structures running in straight lines opposite one another, creating a mall-like path down its center.

Almost immediately, shouts of *"Unjani?* (how are you?) *Juluka"* were directed at Johnny, a long familiar face to the vendors. Here again, we found ourselves not only the lone white patrons, we were practically the only patrons on this Sunday. Johnny told me stories of his youth, how he would come to this place to listen and learn Zulu street guitar from the masters. He expressed more regret at how the violence had brought this once bustling place to its current state, almost empty. People were simply too frightened to come to this Zulu stronghold.

Before we arrived, I asked Johnny if I should attempt my novice isiZulu on the vendors, he said "Absolutely, they will love you for it. White people living HERE don't even try to speak Zulu, they'll love that a white American cares enough to learn it. It's a sign of great respect to them." We started visiting the various shops to check out their wares and to try out my Zulu. All of the shops were small and dark, the only light being that which came through one window and open door. There was a seemingly endless number of *Sangomas* (traditional healers) selling every kind of *muti* (traditional medicines). Some muti shops were filled with racks of glass jars containing traditional herbs, roots and who knows what else. In others, their muti was stored in simple open bins and small containers. Depending on your beliefs, what region you hailed from, and what was wrong with you; sick, in love, or perhaps cursed, you would find the appropriate Sangoma who would then prepare the appropriate muti to fix the problem.

I wish I could have captured on film the faces of the vendors as we entered their proud little shops and I would say, "*Sawubona*", (Hello) or "*Sanibonani*", (Hello to a group.) It was disbelief at first and then pure joy. Smiles have never been broader or more sincere in response to anything I had said to any stranger, any place, at any time. Eyes glistened, and postures became open and inviting as a warm "*Yebo, Sawubona*" came back at me. Not surprisingly, some of my new Acquaintances knew that I was a novice at speaking their language and asked questions in slower than normal pace. "Where are you from?" was the first question. After all, it wasn't every day that a white guy, who wasn't Johnny Clegg, ventured in to their shops speaking Zulu. Once I explained that I came from America, the next question, asked with even greater interest, was "How did you learn to speak Zulu?" I told them I was learning from books and had two "*Abafundisi*" (teachers) who came from KwaZulu Natal and were living in the states. They were very pleased to hear about my teachers.

Johnny and I entered one shop offering beautiful beadwork ornaments and such. I was looking at the various items for sale and realized that Johnny had gone. I thought, "Great, what do I say if the questions go beyond my extremely limited ability?" Thankfully, the ladies asked what were becoming the usual questions. One older woman seated by the door said "*Ukhuluma isiZulu kahle.*" (You speak Zulu well). I had to chuckle and responded "*Ngikhuluma isiZulu njengomntwana*" (I speak Zulu like a child.) That brought laughter and seemed to endear me to them all the more.

As I left the shop in search of Johnny, I nodded respectfully and said *"Salani Kahlè"*, (Stay Well). They smiled and bid me *"Hamba kahlè"* (Go well.) I wasn't more than two-steps out of the door when I heard their voices go in to a happy rapid-fire discussion. No doubt the topic was the customer who just departed their shop. For me, this brief exchange was profound; it reminded me of life in the states, of how people are kept apart as a result of ignorance and fear. Now, here I was in a country where race and ethnicity were threatening civil war and I felt joyful; joyful for having shared smiles and laughter with people I didn't know simply because I was willing to learn something about them.

I found Johnny in a shop a few doors down where the owner sold a wide selection of fighting sticks, cowhide shields and dancing shoes. Johnny picked up a pair of shoes and recited lyrics from one of his songs "he makes dancing shoes from old car tires." Sure enough, the dancing shoes, similar to what we would call *flip-flops*, were indeed made from old tires…the tread still very visible on the soles. The walls of the shop were adorned with a variety of shields; one in particular caught Johnny's attention. It was a small shield made for use by a child, Johnny inquired about its price. R30 (rand) was the answer. He then turned to me, "James, do you have any money?" I had exactly R30. "This would be perfect for Jesse" he said. Jesse was Johnny's three year old son, who one day, would certainly be taught stick fighting and would need such a shield to protect himself. I gladly handed over the R30. The shopkeeper was happy, Johnny was happy and I got to answer all the usual questions one more time.

It was late afternoon by now and Johnny asked if I had any plans for the evening, I did not, so he invited me back to his home for dinner. The drive through the suburbs to his home looked very different from my trips in to Soweto and Vosloorus or even Fluerhof and the Indian part of Johannesburg. These homes, situated on spacious, impeccably manicured lots were large, architecturally impressive, and for the most part, hidden behind high concrete walls. I asked Johnny "what is it with walls everywhere, even in Soweto?" He gave a one word answer "Fear." We turned in to his gently curving drive, behind his high walls and up to the house. The landscaping was perfection, with an assortment of native plants, a lush green lawn and tall trees adorned with wide metal bands around their trunks. "Rats" says Johnny, "they climb up the trees and on to the roof." I couldn't help but look around for the aforementioned invaders; thankfully none were found.

For those of you into architecture and home styling, I confess that I didn't pay much attention to the particulars of the home. I was occupied in conversation as we walked to the house. Inside to greet us was Johnny's mother who was babysitting his son Jesse and visiting for the evening. She was engaging, full of energy, questions and enthusiasm. She made me feel quite at home as Johnny went off to see Jesse. She had been a cabaret singer in her youth and had encouraged Johnny in his love of music from the start. Naturally, she was very proud of him.

Shortly after our arrival Johnny's wife Jenny arrived home. I had met Jenny the previous year backstage at one of Johnny's gigs in Philadelphia and she was very happy that I had finally made it to South Africa. Over a dinner of take-away gyros, the conversation flowed with questions from all sides. Johnny wanted to know which book I was using to study Zulu, I told him, "Learn Zulu." He left the room and returned with an old, well-used copy of the same book I had bought in Hillbrow. "You're learning to speak proper Zulu, not township Zulu" he informed me. When the conversation turned to politics I was thankful for being a student of history and politics because I was asked numerous questions concerning the structure of government in the U.S. How were bills passed? What's the difference between the congress and the senate? Why do some states have more congressmen than others? How could they override a Presidential veto? It was fascinating to see their excitement build as they expressed their hopes for democracy in South Africa.

It was well past 11:00 p.m. when I got back to my room, my mind whirling with thoughts and images of yet another emotionally charged day in South Africa. I turned on the cable TV channel M-Net, watched a film about surfing and waited to hear Charlottie's sweet voice at 3 a.m. On this night, her voice was filled with tears. She was missing me terribly and again questioned why I had to go. Didn't I love her? I had no answers. I could only tell her that I loved her deeply and asked her to please hold on to that thought. Sleep? You must be joking.

Sanity Preserved

While my emotions may have been repeatedly overloaded by the stories of tragedy and pain, they were nurtured back to health through my encounters with musicians I had come to admire, respect and call friends. Blondie and Johnny Clegg of course, but there were so many other memorable meetings. Eleanor Campbell, the executive at Gallo Music, made certain I had access to any of their artists of my choosing. I had already interviewed many of them on the phone; spending time with them in South Africa was pure pleasure. Eleanor did however have one special surprise that she held back. She stopped by my hotel early one morning to tell me she had something planned for that evening and to "bring your tape recorder."

There was little time to try and figure out what she might have planned, because shortly after she left I was collected by a sales rep from another record label. He was making sales calls to small shops in surrounding townships. These were *Mom and Pop* stores that sold LPs and cassettes in addition to household goods, groceries, clothing and just about anything else a township resident might need. Some of the shops were only slightly fancier than the makeshift Spaza shops you find throughout the townships. Today's territory included Katlehong, Thokoza, Zonkiziswe and Vosloorus.

Even after numerous trips into the townships, I continued to be struck by the images I was seeing. Just as they had done in Soweto, our travels took us through every imaginable level of poverty and wealth, all squashed in together. Dressed in an impeccable gray suit, Henry, his Christian name, possessed an impressive command of several languages. This came in handy as we visited shops run by Xhosa, Zulu, Sotho and Venda speaking proprietors. He didn't talk much in the way of politics as we drove on; expect to say he wished that the violence would come to an end sooner than later. This statement of hope was followed by a noticeable shrug and "we shall see."

Henry's relationship with his clients was relaxed and friendly. Many were more than a bit surprised when he showed up with a white man in tow. A quick explanation and it was smiles all round. While Henry did his sales thing, I poked around the shops. When he came to collect me at the hotel that morning, Henry provided an interesting lesson in ethnic profiling. As we were walking across the lobby, two women from housekeeping approached, Henry nodded and said, "*Sanibonani*" (hello). They replied "*Yebo, Sanibonani.*" When they had passed, I asked, "How did you know those women were Zulu?" Without hesitation he said, "Oh, you can just tell."

That evening Eleanor picked me up at 6:30 sharp, still refusing to tell me what she had planned. She drove us out to the posh suburb of Rosebank and pulled up to valet parking at an impressive looking restaurant. Was dinner the "something special"? I admit to feeling a bit confused. If dinner was the big surprise, why bring my recorder? She had reservations and the hostess brought us to a table right in front of a small stage. "Okay" I thought, "so they have a band here, cool." Before we sat down, we were approached by a short gray haired African man dressed in a deep purple, tie-dyed tunic and black pants; he looked very familiar, but only a little.

Eleanor said, "James, I'd like you to meet Ntemi Piliso." I was floored. Eleanor continued, "The African Jazz Pioneers are playing tonight." For me, as well as an endless number of jazz fans in South Africa and across Europe, Ntemi Piliso is a living legend, a musical giant, on par with any great bandleader you'd care to name. He was one of the pioneers, who in the 1950s, melded American big band and *Marabi* jazz, a style born in townships, to create a sound unique to South Africa. With Ntemi at the helm, the 11 member African Jazz Pioneers were keeping that sound alive and turning on a new generation to a rich musical culture that is all their own. Ntemi was a bit surprised at my enthusiastic reaction to meeting him, and to my expectation of hearing the Pioneers play. Yes, I was star-struck and couldn't stop smiling. Eleanor took us off to a side table where I could interview him before they went on.

For the benefit of my listeners, Ntemi spoke about *Marabi* and the Pioneers. "There is the western influence of big bands, but that doesn't mean it is western, the fact is, it's African, not the most indigenous, but it's African." Ntemi felt strongly about "maintaining that African sound." When asked about the *discovery* of Marabi by whites, Ntemi was "very surprised, because in the 50's they wouldn't listen to it. I think maybe we were not given a chance to play the music for them, because the laws were not allowing us to do that."

He told stories of the funky shebeens where he played in the early days, including the legendary township of Sophiatown, destroyed under the Natives Resettlement Act of 1954 to make way for the white suburb of *Triomf*, Afrikaans for Triumph. "Sophiatown was a very lively location, yes, one of the liveliest I can think of. The environment was nice because everything happened there." He was soft-spoken, humble, but at the same time, rightfully proud and passionate about his music. The interview concluded and it was show time. Who could think about dinner? The band sounded better than any recording of theirs I had heard. Tight, melodic and African to the core, I was in heaven and Eleanor just sat back and smiled at my delight. The arrangements were designed to let everyone in the band shine, seamlessly flowing from one solo to the next. How do you describe that almost spiritual feeling you get when music completely envelopes you?

It took several numbers before I realized that I was the most ecstatic member of the audience. There was applause, but it was polite and heard amidst clinking of glasses and utensils. Were these people deaf? Did they not realize this was a national treasure before them? During the break, Eleanor brought the lone female member of the band to our table. "James, this is Jennifer Klot; Jennifer, tell James where you're from." Jennifer smiled and said;"New Jersey!" At the urging of a friend, Jennifer came to South Africa where she met Ntemi at a club in Johannesburg and landed a gig with the Pioneers. She came from north Jersey and wasn't too familiar with the Philadelphia or south Jersey area, but it hardly mattered; it was a wonderful link to home hearing a Jersey/New York accent in suburban Johannesburg…. plus, she played one hell of a sax.

The second set was more electrifying than the first. The band was loose, having a great time and the music pouring out of them effortlessly. My mind was carried away from the thoughts and visions born out of the many days of emotional trauma. Eleanor continued to smile at my delight; she knew that for me, this was a memorable evening. Just this year I reconnected with Jennifer who now lives in New York and she confirmed everything I felt about Ntemi; kind, gentle and passionate about his music. Ntemi passed away in December of 2000 at the age of 75. Bless his soul.

There were other nights when live music helped to preserve my sanity; Sipho graciously provided those. Many daytime hours were happily spent in the company of some of my favorite musicians; several would become friends. Thanks to the record label executives who believed in what I was doing, these artists welcomed me to South Africa with open arms. I was especially moved by Sipho Gumede, a world-class bassist in the band Sakhile and a very gentle, creative soul. After numerous phone conversations, we finally met face to face at the Mega Music Complex in Newtown, he embraced me saying, "Welcome home James!" A few years after the radio program ended, and I felt wasted and down, Sipho phoned me at home just to check on how I was doing. It was heartbreaking news that came my way in July 2004, Sipho died of lung cancer at the age of 47.

During one long afternoon interview session in which I was meeting a number of artists, I sat with the beautiful Nelcy Sedibe and watched her latest video. The music had a contemporary, yet very African groove. The video opened with spectacular visuals shot in neighboring Swaziland, her country of birth. As I was getting in to the music and visuals, the giant video screen was filled with a shot of a topless Nelcy. I've seen topless women in videos before, but I have never had any of the women sitting next to me while I watched. I kept my eyes straight ahead, locked to the screen. Nelcy chuckled and said, "Typical Swazi, we let it all hang out." I heard myself say, "You're very beautiful." I'm still not certain if I said that out loud or to myself.

Later that evening, I returned to the record label offices to attend a party celebrating yet another gold LP for the legendary Soul Brothers. Considered by many to be the most successful recording artists in South African history, the Soul Brothers racked up record sales in the millions. Their infectious township rhythms are propelled by Moses Ngwenya on organ, and sweetened by vocalist David Masondo. Their lyrics, exclusively in Zulu, speak to the hearts of the people, telling tales of love, the hardship of life under apartheid, loss of loved ones and of the belief of a brighter future. A Soul Brothers concert is a sensory treat for the eyes and ears; a full band pulling you from your seat with driving force and David's vocals strengthened by no less than 4 male backing vocalists who incorporate extraordinary dance routines to the groove. This band set the standard by which all imitators are judged.

When I arrived at the labels' reception room it was already crowded with members of the press and invited guests. I was greeted warmly by Liz, the label rep; the same Liz who initially hated my choice of the word *Amandla* for my program. Thankfully, she was now an ardent supporter. Liz brought me over to meet Moses and David before things got underway. I had spoken to Moses a few times on the phone and was quite happy to finally meet him face to face and to meet David as well.

In the few moments leading up to the award ceremony, the label chief approached me asking, "You speak Zulu right?" I informed him that I was "learning" to speak Zulu and still spoke like a child. He seemed unfazed by this response and continued, "We want you to introduce Moses and David and speak a little Zulu when you do; the people will love it!" I said that I would be honored to introduce the guys, but he is quite insane to think that I would attempt to speak Zulu here and now. He insisted and promised me it would make a great impression. I was thinking, "Impression? No shit, I'll look and sound like an idiot", an impression I'd rather not make.

Too late, before I could convince him otherwise I found myself in front of the microphone.

I had no trouble explaining who I was and why I was in South Africa; many of the assembled already knew me, then came the Zulu bit. Somehow, someway I heard myself flawlessly stating "I love the Soul Brothers, and my listeners in Philadelphia love the Soul Brothers very much!" Not exactly the Zulu equivalent of Shakespeare, but what the hell, I was LEARNING! As the last words were leaving my lips I saw big smiles and heard loud applause. For once in my life, I couldn't wait to get away from the microphone. Moses and David came up to the mic and were presented with beautifully framed gold LP's; photos were taken and they humbly thanked everyone for attending. They had performed this ritual many times before and would certainly be doing it many more times in the future.

At one point during the evening, Alex Rantselli and his brother Marc arrived at the party. I had met Alex on the roadside during my tour of Soweto with Blondie. While his brother mingled, Alex and I chatted about their latest CD, slated to be released in the U.S. the next month. I had received an advance copy and simply hated it. The U.S. record label had remixed the original tracks to appeal to western ears. All of the driving instrumentation and backing rhythm tracks that made it African were gone. Alex asked my opinion and I withheld nothing "I think it's horrible. They stripped it of everything African, everything that made it great." Alex looked down for a moment shaking his head from side to side and said "Thank you! They DID fuck it up!" He then called Marc over to join us.

Alex introduced me as the American DJ he had spoken of and then instructed Marc to "ask James what he thinks of our U.S. release." This time I chose to use Alex's words, "They fucked it up," I said. Marc's eyes grew big, he grabbed me by both arms, tilted his head back and said "Thank you" in full agreement. They told me that their South African label was a division of the larger U.S. label and that they had "no say" in how the CD would be remixed for U.S. consumption. Both of them were extremely disappointed in the outcome and felt that their first venture in to the U.S. market would fail miserably; they were correct.

The remained of the evening was spent talking with other guests, answering questions about the radio program, about the things I had seen and done since my arrival, and what I thought about the current state of things in South Africa. We all knew that the fairy-tale ending was far from certain; there was plenty of pain and bloodshed still to come.

The Old Man

My final full day in South Africa began just as the preceding days before it, lying in my bed wide awake and watching the bluish-gray light of dawn creep in through my window. After 14 intense days, some mind-numbingly emotional, and some filled with pure joy, this was supposed to be a downtime day. The only real plan included a visit to the Joubert Park section of the city to see Sipho's new office and walk a number of blocks to visit the Mecca of South African record stores, Kohinoor. For decades, this humble shop was the destination for anyone, white, black or colored, in search of hard to find jazz, rhythm and blues and Motown recordings. Vinyl was Kohinoor's stock and trade and even with the advent of the CD, Kohinoor maintained their *vinyl only* inventory.

There was one addition to my day that I would never have thought possible, thanks to Colin my friend from the Open School. Earlier in the week, Colin stopped by my hotel for a quick visit. He had come to invite me to an ANC rally on Saturday night, my last night in South Africa. The rally would be held in the *colored* area of Riverlea, just outside of Soweto; the featured speaker was Nelson Mandela. Many in the so-called colored community feared that they would be marginalized, excluded if you will, by the mostly black ANC when they came to power.

Mandela, along with other speakers, was hoping to ease their anxiety. As a result of his position within the local chapter of the ANC, Colin would be on-stage with Mandela and the other dignitaries. In addition, my friend and host, Blondie Makhene and his group Amaqabane were scheduled to warm up the crowd before the speeches with a live performance. Of course I said yes, I would be honored to attend.

When I told Colin of my plans for the daytime portion of my last Saturday, he suggested that since I would be in Joubert Park, why not stop by Shell House, the headquarters of the ANC. Great idea! I expressed to him my hope of perhaps meeting Barbara Masekela, we had never met face to face, and I wanted to thank her for her support during her tenure as head of the ANC's Cultural Desk. Now, she was Chief of Staff to ANC President Nelson Mandela. I really wasn't expecting to see her; she had enormous responsibilities in her new role and certainly wouldn't have the time. Colin smiled at this and said, "I know Barbara very well, let's see what we can do."

He picked up the hotel room phone, dialed, and in a few moments said, "Barbara Mesekela please." Shortly Barbara came on the line and Colin told her that I was in South Africa and wanted to stop by to pay a visit. She thought that it would be wonderful to spend some time with me first thing in the morning.

Then, Colin hit her with what I thought to be a ridiculous request. "James is coming to Riverlea Saturday night; do you think you could get him time with Madiba?" This was pushing it, so I wasn't surprised at her answer. "His schedule is very tight that night, I can't guarantee anything." I wasn't disappointed in the least, I wanted to meet Barbara and felt that just seeing Mandela in a small township hall in South Africa was more than I ever expected from this trip.

So here we are, Saturday morning and I set out from my room for my last day of adventure in Johannesburg. Since my destination was too far to walk, I had to order a taxi to get me there. That meant dealing with the racist reception clerk for what would be the next to the last time. I knew this was going to be one of those moments when a candid photograph would be priceless. As I approached the desk she spotted me and quickly went from doing nothing, to looking down seemingly engrossed in something very urgent. I stood at the desk and waited for her to finish her imaginary responsibility. Finally, she looked up, not speaking a word. I asked her to please phone for a taxi. Staying true to form she said, "I'm not going to call one of those *black* taxis, they're simply not safe. The colored ones are alright though." Even taxi service was a racial issue with this woman. She picked up the receiver and dialed, looked at me and asked, "Where do you need to go?" Oh, how sweet the memory of her face. "To Plein Street." Her eyes locked on to mine, I could almost see the images racing through her mind.

Plein Street! Blacks, terrorists, murderers, danger! I paused for a moment: her mouth fell open as I added "the ANC offices at Shell House." Guilty as charged for allowing my mischievous side to get the better of me. I simply wanted to piss her off one more time. Once she regained her usual cheerful composure, she informed the colored taxi service where to deliver me, hung up the receiver and said nothing more. After thanking her with an exaggerated smile, I went to wait outside. A short while later I found myself in the back seat, taking my very first ride in a safe and secure *colored* taxi. We were scarcely 100 yards from the hotel when the driver asked, "Why are you going to visit the ANC?" I hesitated for a moment, debating with myself about how detailed a response to provide; based on what I had learned during my visit, I knew that politics was a volatile, sometimes dangerous subject.

"Fuck it" as Jiggs would say, I chose to tell him everything, the radio program, why I was in South Africa, who I knew and more. He listened intently as he drove. When I finished he said, "I think what you are doing is a very good thing. It's very bad in this country right now. We need Mandela and the ANC to change things." It wasn't a long ride, but it was quite a pleasant one, providing the opportunity to connect with yet another hopeful soul in a troubled land. He pulled the taxi over to the curb and announced, "Shell House." I got out, paid the fare and gladly handed him an extra-large tip, shook his hand and wished him well.

A collection of office buildings, various stores and small shops, along with canopy covered sidewalks make up this section of Plein Street. Shell House stood in the middle of its block, all 22 stories of it. Upon entering, you are presented with a choice of going to the lobby area to the right where ANC comrades were assisting current members and signing up new ones, or you can continue to the information desk and security entrance straight ahead, that was my destination. The very polite, very well dressed information attendant asked how he may assist me and I told him I was there to meet Barbara Masekela. "Thank you sir" he said. He looked down at the log book on the desk in front of him, looked up and said "Please go to the security entrance sir and they will direct you from there, have a good visit." I made my way to the security area of the main lobby; it resembled the passenger screening areas at major airports; full body scan and a physical search of all packages, bags and equipment you may be carrying. The security team member who motioned for me to approach was quite courteous almost to the extreme as he searched my shoulder bag containing my tape recorder, mic, cassettes and camera.

This screening process was the complete opposite of the interrogation I had gone through at Jan Smuts Airport. As he completed his search, he asked who I was coming to meet, I told him Barbara Masekela, he smiled, told me on which floor to find "Comrade Barbara" and wished me "a good visit, sir." "How amazing was this?" I asked myself as I rode the elevator up to meet Barbara.

Just 18 months ago the ANC was an illegal organization, declared to be terrorists, and now they're headquartered in a 22-story office building in downtown Johannesburg! The elevator doors opened on to a small reception area where an impeccably dressed male staff member greeted me. For former terrorists, these guys sure know how to dress. He asked for, and I produced my passport and informed him that I had come to meet with Barbara.

After a quick phone call to announce my arrival, another staff member came to collect me. He escorted me a short distance past offices and desks and in to Barbara's private office where she was waiting. With close cropped hair, eyeglass and beautifully tailor brown suit, Barbara was the epitome of the professional, 40-something African woman; and yes, you could immediately see the resemblance to older brother Hugh. I had seen photos and spoken with her so many times it made this first meeting warm and familiar, just as it had been with others I had met during this visit. Barbara was filled with questions about my visit and the progress of my radio program. I was filled with questions about her exciting new role as Chief of Staff and all that had transpired. "We've been so very busy, we've hardly had time to take it all in" was her reply. She kindly introduced me to staff members, while praising my work. I was flattered and somewhat embarrassed.

Here I was with people who had lived most of their lives in exile or under of the oppression of apartheid and Barbara was praising my work. Then she totally took me by surprise when she asked, "Would you like to meet the old man?" The Old Man? I had to smile, I knew that Mandela was called Madiba, his clan name, and I had also heard him called "The Chief", but "The Old Man?" It spoke volumes about how Mandela viewed himself, he was just another loyal member of the ANC, and he knew that "Old Man" was spoken with respect and admiration, a title I believe he wore proudly. "I would like that very much." Really, who would say "No"? Barbara excused herself and went to collect *the Old Man*.

During her absence, I considered what I would say, mildly worried that I would be nervous and stammer my way through this once in a lifetime opportunity. Before I had time to ramp up my nervousness to a fever pitch, Barbara reappeared at the door, hand-in-hand with a smiling Nelson Mandela. The affection shared between these two was endearing. It reminded me of a father, proudly standing beside his daughter on the day of her wedding. As I walked over to join them Barbara introduced me "This is Comrade James Eoppolo who is doing great work for us in Philadelphia." I was honored by the introduction. As we shook hands, Mandela smiled broadly and welcomed me to South Africa. *The embodiment of dignity.*

That was my immediate impression. I was also struck by the fact that I felt no pangs of nervousness, I was completely at ease with this living, breathing icon of the struggle. He was somehow regal and yet, you could sense that he considered himself to be just another comrade working toward a shared goal, and accepted me as someone doing the same.

He inquired about my visit and listened intently to my answers, his brilliant, twinkling eyes locked on to mine. There was never a moment when I felt that he wasn't listening to every word I said, or that he wanted to cut short this conversation. In later years I would read and hear that most everyone who met him felt the same. I mentioned that I was looking forward to his speech that night in Riverlea; and he related his strong feelings of wanting to ally the fears of the colored community, to make certain that they felt welcomed in the ANC and in the new government, whenever that would come to be. We shook hands once again and Barbara invited me to be seated in her office.

She took Mandela's hand in hers and escorted him down the hall. As I sat at the small desk waiting for her return, I thought that this visit to my adopted homeland could not have come to a better end. Barbara returned shortly, sat down behind her desk and casually asked, "So, James, what do you have planned for the rest of the day?" My itinerary was simple; a walk to Kohinoor Record Store and a stop off at Sipho's office around the corner. She gave a nod of acknowledgement as she spoke, "If you can come back around noon the Chief can give you 15 minutes for a private interview." Trying not to look overly stunned by this remarkable invitation, I assured Barbara that I would make myself available at whatever time suited Madiba. She then suggested that I write down a series of topics that I would like to cover, this would afford "the Old Man" an brief opportunity to prepare. Barbara excused herself for a moment, leaving me to face an immense challenge.

How do you whittle down several thousand questions to a precious few? Since my radio program dealt with culture's role in the struggle, that topic was a must; followed by his thoughts on the escalating violence and who was behind it. There was heated debate concerning the lifting of sanctions against South Africa, so that made the list as well. Upon her return, I presented Barbara with a half dozen topics for discussion and hoped that I had chosen wisely. Barbara escorted me back to the elevators, instructing me to return at noon.

I was to go to the reception desk in the lobby and inform them that I had an appointment with "The Chief". She then expressed her regret that due to other priorities, she would be unable to join us in Riverlea that night. The ride down to the lobby was done in a bit of a daze. I had arrived with the intention of saying hello to Barbara, and was now leaving with a private meeting scheduled with Nelson Mandela! I had to consciously keep myself from running out of Shell House and dashing the few blocks to Sipho's office.

Like me, he was ecstatic at this amazing opportunity and demanded a full report after the interview. With about an hour and a half to kill, I headed out from Sipho's office for Kohinoor Record Store several blocks away. This would be a good time to clear my head and rehearse my interview questions. As I made my way down the busy streets toward my destination, a rather surprising revelation overtook me; I was the only white person around! This was an incredible sensation, one that I had never experienced in my life. No wonder African-Americans love visiting Africa, the minority becomes the majority. This wondrous discovery put a bounce in my step, I felt proud to be among these people who were on the brink of historic change. I smiled to think of how my overtly racist, doom and gloom predicting hotel receptionist would fare in this sea of blackness.

She would simply die from fear, end of story. Before I knew it, I was stepping inside Kohinoor and flipping through row after row of jazz, R & B and soul recordings, all on good old vinyl. I confess to being somewhat disappointed at the overall selection, especially when you compared it to U.S. record stores. Still, when you factor in where you are, it's easy to understand how Kohinoor earned its reputation as the Mecca of record stores in South Africa. While reading liner notes and exploring record bins was a great distraction, I kept my eye on the time. There was no way that I would allow even a moment of delay.

Relaxed and confident was my mood as I re-entered Shell House. I approached the information desk and announced that I had a noontime meeting with President Mandela. The young comrade behind the desk smiled politely and said "I'm sorry sir, but the chief is not in the building."

Trying not to reveal the panic that began chewing at my insides, I then asked for Barbara Masekela, figuring she could straighten out this little mix-up.

"I'm sorry sir, but Comrade Barbara is out for the remainder of the day."

"Shit!" I screamed in my mind, trying to remain calm. "Do you know if the President is due back anytime soon? Barbara set up this meeting for noon." He shook his head and told me that "The Chief was out at a meeting, he should have been back, but I don't know what caused the delay."

He then invited me to have a seat; he would let me know the minute The Chief returned. I sat off to the side and tried to console myself with the fact that at least I was able to spent time with him in Barbara's office. It helped, but not for long. Five minutes turned in to ten, then fifteen. As I waited, people drifted in and out asking questions about joining the ANC, which branch meetings they should attend and so forth. At the half hour mark of my agony, I was pretty well convinced that fate had played its hand, there would be no meeting. "Comrade. Excuse me, comrade." The attendant manning the information desk was talking to me, but I was so engrossed in thought I barely heard him. I looked in his direction, he smiled and said "Comrade, The Chief in back, you can go up." I tried to remain cool and not explode off of my chair. I got up calmly, thanked him for his kindness and passed through the security checkpoint.

As before, the elevator opened on the same small reception area and two gentlemen were there to greet me. They already knew who I was and why I was there. We proceeded in the same direction as if going to Barbara's office, but continued further down the hall. There in the door, waiting was Nelson Mandela. He smiled that disarming smile and shook my hand. I said "Madiba, I wish to thank you for…." Mandela raised his hand as if to stop me, "Barbara has told me all that you are doing for my people, and it is I, who should be thanking you."

It wasn't until much later that night while alone in my hotel room did I have time to contemplate this short exchange and what it meant to me. I had a job to do and the calmness that I felt upon our first meeting had thankfully returned. I followed Mandela in to his office. The room was by no means lavish; in fact it was quite simple. One or two not so very memorable prints on the wall, his large wooden desk just inside facing the door; off to his left a small octagonal desk for meetings. There was also an emergency escape door near the meeting desk. What was beyond it, I will never know. He motioned for me to take a seat while he tidied up some paperwork on his desk. My only bout with nerves came as I plugged in my mic, checked the level on my tape recorder and prayed like holy hell that this recording would be flawless. Mandela came over and sat beside me and gave a nod that he was ready whenever I was. I pressed the red "RECORD" button, said another silent prayer and began the interview.

My first question was on the topic of culture and the vital role it played during the darkest years of apartheid, when leaders were in prison or in exile. I asked if he and his many comrades were aware of this while on Robben Island. He thought for a moment and replied, 'The cultural community in South Africa has always played a creative role in maintaining the identity of our people. Indeed it has been a medium through which, in the face of an unprecedented assault on their collective psyche; our people have derived a particular strength and optimism about a better future."

He spoke slowly, thoughtfully, choosing his words carefully; punctuating key words and always looking straight in to my eyes. He continued, "Perhaps the most touching performances of South African music has been the freedom songs composed in jails, camps and the streets of struggle. The uniqueness of these plaintive tunes tinged with sadness and joy, strength and beauty have captured the spirit of our people alive." With the *fluff* question now out of the way, I moved on to the so-called "black on black" violence. His features grew very stern. "Up to the time of the signing of the Peace Accord, the de Klerk government has been conniving at the violence. But what is even more serious…they have gone further, because the state security services themselves have been deeply involved in the slaughtering of our people."

I had heard and read accounts of just how angry Mandela had become with de Klerk over the state's involvement in fueling the violence. The look on his face and the serious tone in his voice brought home the point. "The state security services have also organized various shapes of death squads, like the so-called Koevoet and Battalion 32. All these people have been involved in fueling this violence. So, Mr. de Klerk has up until the signing of the Peace Accord been deeply involved in the violence."

After his release, many world leaders were calling for an end to all sanctions imposed on South Africa; again, Mandela had strong feelings about these suggestions. "The proper thing to do is to maintain sanctions. It is not true that we have reached a stage when we can say the process of reform has become irreversible." He paused for a moment, and with a sweeping motion of his hand continued "Nothing can be irreversible until the masses of the people themselves are able to defend democratic changes. That moment will only come when blacks are in power." He was quite animated as he went on, "When we are members of parliament, when we, by virtue of the vote can then use that parliament for the purpose of defending those democratic changes." In case there was any doubt about his position on the topic, he stated it clearly, "It is an illusion to talk of us having reached a stage where we no longer need sanctions, we need them." I asked him to share his thoughts on the way the western press was now covering South Africa, as if all things had been resolved. He felt as if "a large sector of the press was not presenting the situation correctly" but hoped that their attitude would soon change.

My fifteen minutes were almost up; I wrapped things up by inviting him to Philadelphia upon his return to the states. He assured me that "we will take the first opportunity to visit Philadelphia so that we can thank the people directly for the support they have given us over the years."

And with that, my private meeting with Nelson Mandela came to a conclusion. He escorted me to the door of his office, shook my hand, thanked me for my work in Philadelphia and instructed his aide to "Please escort Comrade James out." The aide brought me back to the reception area and even phoned a taxi to take me back to my hotel. I couldn't help wonder if he was calling a *black* taxi or a colored one. As it turned out, it was another *colored* taxi and the driver was ecstatic when I told him that I had just interviewed Madiba.

When I arrived back to the hotel I couldn't resist looking directly at *the bitch* and smiling ear to ear as I walked by. In return she gave me her customary "I wish you were dead" glare. All was right in the world. Since I was flying out early the next morning and would be out very late that night, I decided to make good use of my time and pack everything that wouldn't be needed in the next eighteen hours. Before any of that, I needed to check my taped interview with Madiba; I didn't have the time to do that at Shell House nor in the backseat of the taxi. I pressed REWIND and nervously waited as the tape whirled its way backward. Click. Then, with my guts in a knot, I pressed PLAY. There was my brief mic check. That sounded okay; a short pause...and finally the interview itself. It sounded fine from start to finish. I allowed myself to listen to it twice, then removed the cassette and hid it beneath my bed; figuring, that if all of my things were suddenly stolen on my last day, at least I could bring back my most important recording.

I phoned my wife to tell her what had just transpired, going in to my promotional mode as well; asking her to alert the Philadelphia press that I was returning with an exclusive interview with Nelson Mandela, a coveted trophy that no other journalist in the city had yet won. I was constantly trying to build and maintain credibility for the radio program; thanks to Colin and Barbara, my private interview with Madiba provided the ultimate stamp of approval.

Around 4:00 pm Blondie and his wife Agnes came by to collect me in the company kombi. We headed off for a last night's dinner together before picking up Blondie's friend Connie, along with his wife and twin boys. Connie had accompanied us on my first visit in to Soweto and being *colored* was naturally keen to hear Mandela's speech as well. It was quite dark by the time we arrived in the township of Riverlea outside of Soweto; so I never got to *see* much of it. Blondie and Connie explained that Riverlea is yet another exceedingly poor area populated by those "who believe that they do not fit in, neither black nor white. They already feel marginalized. That's why tonight is so important"

Blondie swung the long kombi in to a parking space beside the township hall. We filed out, made our way through the crowd that was chanting, singing and toyi-toying outside and headed in to the low, wide building. Blondie went backstage to prepare and we sat about five rows back from the stage.

The hall held about two-hundred people and knowing that it would fill up quickly, loudspeakers were set up outside for the convenience of those who couldn't get in. The stage was practically as wide as the hall itself. The speaker's podium was situated to the far left. A row of chairs for the dignitaries and huge ANC and Communist Party banners held center stage. Camera crews from the government run SABC were present, as well as a bevy of photographers. Mandela had only been out of prison for eighteen months and for many South Africans he was still a mythical figure, seen only on their TV sets. This would be the first time that he would address the concerns of the colored community in such a direct fashion and it was big news. If the ANC couldn't win the support of the colored voters, they might not win an election.

I brought my camera and tape recorder along to capture the moment and felt honored to be present at this historic moment. The hall was packed to capacity; a sense of excited anticipation began to build. Connie told me that Mandela really needed pull out all the stops to capture the hearts of these people or it could be bad news for the ANC. He also told me that as a sign of respect, Mandela will probably speak Afrikaans most of the time. Thanks to the apartheid education system, Afrikaans is the primary language of most of the colored population. It was a just after 8:00 when Blondie and his group Amaqabane took the stage. They were going to sing to a prerecorded music track from their new album.

The music kicked in and the crowd went out of control. Many jumped from their seats took to the aisle and started the toyi-toyi, literally rocking the building. Connie turned to me with a wide grin and said "That Blondie is a fucking genius!" He was right. As Blondie sang a struggle song, which lambasted one of Pretoria's puppet leaders, the toyi-toying crowd waved ANC flags and chanted along. The camera crews loved it! When Blondie finished shouts of "Amandla!" and "ANC" reverberated through the hall. Out came the two key-note speakers, Mandela, and the Reverend Allan Boesak, who at the time was a highly respected, *colored* anti-apartheid leader. Years later he would fall from grace thanks to charges of misappropriation of funds. Then, out came the dignitaries, including Colin "Jiggs" Smuts, looking very dapper in a dark red shirt and tie, Peter whom I had met at the Open School, plus a few others.

Peter gave a short introduction regarding the reason for this town hall meeting and then introduced the man everyone had come to see and hear. Nelson Mandela took to the podium amidst thunderous applause. Despite this overwhelming welcome, it was clear that this crowd wanted some concise answers from this man. They were willing to listen, but he had better deliver. Right off, he started out speaking in Afrikaans and you could see from the faces of the crowd that he was quickly making a connection.

Just as he had always done, Mandela spoke slowly, punctuating key words and phrases. The crowd responded with applause and at times, laughter. Connie would lean toward me and tried to quickly translate the humor, but he didn't want to miss a word, so I never *really* understood the jokes.

After a slight pause, he switched to English; speaking of inclusiveness for all the people, and of the ANC's vision for a truly non-racial, democratic South Africa. He timed his transitions from language to language perfectly. I think the English bit was mostly for the assembled press from all over. At one point during another segment in Afrikaans, I asked Connie his opinion of how Mandela was doing. "He's saying all the right things. He is saying that he understands their frustrations that the ANC will never abandon them. He's doing great!" As he finished his speech it was evident that Mandela did exactly what Connie thought, the crowd cheered and chanted wildly. Mandela bowed graciously and took his seat on the stage as just another member of the ANC.

A few other speeches followed, driving home the point that the colored community had a home in the ANC. The evening concluded with everyone standing as Blondie came out to sing the anthem *Nkosi Sikelel' iAfrika*. I'm not certain if it was due to my two weeks of sleep deprivation or the events that filled my time; but throughout the entire evening I felt as if I was living in a dream state.

I had dedicated the last five years reading, listening, living and breathing all things South African, and on this single day, I had spent private time with Nelson Mandela and was now in a township hall singing *Nkosi Sikelel' iAfrika* with him and several hundred passionate citizens. As it always does the anthem/prayer ends with the shout *"Amandla!" (Power!),* and the crowd answers *"Awethu!"* (*Is ours!).* Then, *"Mayibuye!"* (*Let it return!),* the crowd responds *"iAfrika!"* The event was over. As the crowd filed out, singing, chanting and toyi-toying, Colin came from backstage to find me. He asked, "would you like to come back to have coffee and cakes with Madiba and just a few people from tonight?" Can this incredible day possibly continue?

We headed back to the small reception room where a simple folding table was set with coffee and cakes. Blondie and a few of the others from on stage were present. There, standing at the table was Madiba. He turned and spotted me, walked straight toward me and with a smile asked,

"So, James, how did you enjoy your last day in our country?" Temporarily dumbfounded, I thought, how did Nelson Mandela remember my name? This man has a nation to save and he is able to remember *my* name? We shook hands and I told him that he made my last day truly memorable. Colin, who by now knew that we had met two times earlier in the day asked, "Did you get your picture taken with Madiba?"

My answer was "No, I hadn't because it was just he and I alone in his office." Colin took my camera handed it to his son Themba saying, "Let's get a shot of the two of you!"

After quickly instructing Themba on the use of my camera I stepped back beside Madiba. Themba aimed, pressed the shutter and...nothing. No click, no flash, nothing! Thinking that the photo was taken, Madiba began to move away. In the milliseconds that followed, it hit me that I had spent time with one of the most important people of the century and had no visual record of it...shit!! I blurt out that the picture wasn't taken, please try again. I tried not to shout at Themba,

"You have to press and hold the button down."

Thankfully, Madiba understood the problem, stopped and moved back to my side. Once again Themba raised the camera, pointed, pressed and held the button down. The camera clicked, the flash went off and I instantly heard the sound of the camera motor rewinding. It was the very last frame of my very last roll of film. My stomach sank like a stone.

As I thanked Madiba for his remarkable kindness, I remembered the universal truth that ninety-nine point nine percent of the time, the last picture on a roll of film NEVER comes out. What the hell, I knew that this evening, this day, this journey would be burned in to my soul forever, with or without the picture.

If you'll forgive my jumping forward, I will tell you that upon my return home the staff at my local camera shop could not locate any of the film that I had dropped off for developing. Twenty-four excruciating hours later they phoned to tell me that they had found my photos. I raced over to retrieve them, never expecting to see the one photo that was on top of the stack. It was Nelson Mandela and me!

I spent the remainder of my time at the gathering chatting with a few of the other guests, including Reverend Boesak. I really liked this guy. He was young, hip, very quick witted and a major player in the movement. It was a relaxed chat about how well the evening had gone, the continued struggle, and the unenviable task of following Madiba on stage. I had seen, heard and read about Reverend Boesak more times than I could count, and here I was in a South African township hall having coffee and cakes with him. Surreal.

After our chat, he asked Colin to give him a lift back to his hotel. Colin urged me to join them. It was getting late and I figured now was as good a time as any to bring this day to an end. I went over to Blondie and told him that Colin was going to drop me off at my hotel. I embraced him and thanked him for making this life changing visit possible.

Blondie repeated his reasons for bringing me to South Africa and instructed me to "go back and tell Philadelphia and the U.S. the truth about what is happening here." Vowing to do just that, we parted. Riding in a car with Colin at the wheel was an adventure the first time he took me to dinner, so I knew I was in for a wild excursion back to my hotel. He's one of those drivers who like to look at you as they talk. While I agree that eye contact helps drive home a point, whizzing through city streets while doing it takes a master orator/driver. That, my friend, would be Colin.

Racing through Riverlea, and then in to Jo'burg; he, Allan and I were talking up a storm; Colin looking at Allan and even turning to look at me in the backseat. Somehow, buses, cars, kombis and pedestrians were all miraculously avoided. We deposited Allan at the entrance to his posh hotel and a short time later found ourselves parked in front of my considerably more humble, considerably more racist digs in Berea. I offered Colin my endless thanks for his humor, the dinner, the booze and for making my personal *Madiba Day* possible. He laughed with a snort and said that he was "fucking glad to do it." That was much appreciated. Off he went.

Walking through the lobby and past the front desk on my way to the elevator, I thought about requesting a wake up call; that thought process lasted about three seconds. No way in hell was I going to trust *the bitch* to actually wake me in time for a 7:15 a.m. flight. Then again, maybe she'd be willing to drive me to the airport just to be rid of me once and for all! I chose to set my own alarm, not that I expected to get any sleep. I finished my last bit of packing, set my alarm for 5:00 a.m. and chuckled at the fact that after Charlottie's 3:00 a.m. phone call, I'd only have two hours to kill before the alarm did its thing. Knowing full well that I would be awake anyway, I debated about setting it at all, but I wanted to go home badly and wasn't about to risk missing my flight. This last night alone was the toughest of any I had spent in South Africa. It was as though several months of intense emotional upheaval were crammed in to the past two weeks, and I was finding it difficult to quiet the flood of thoughts vying for my attention. I flipped on the TV, tried to calm myself and waited for Charlottie's call. When she rang me I was still wired. I told her about the rally, the coffee and cakes with Madiba, the picture that probably wouldn't come out and how desperately I wanted to come home. Yes, I loved visiting South Africa, and yes, I fell in love with its people, but I needed to decompress, and to do that. I needed to be with her, to be home. Of course we heard the usual click and drop in volume during our call. Before we hung up, I felt obliged to say goodbye to our eavesdropping friends. I told them to "go fuck themselves", told my wife "I love you" and we rang off. That felt good.

Homeward Bound…Almost

At 4:55 a.m. I rose from my fitful hour or so of sleep, showered, arranged my bags, checked my room for anything forgotten and headed down to the lobby to arrange for a taxi to take me to Jan Smuts Airport. Sipho had talked about taking me, but I felt that he had done enough for me already. We said goodbye at his office the previous day, with each of us feeling more determined than ever to make the radio program meaningful. As I dragged my now heavier than ever bags across the lobby floor, I was faced with one last duel with Miss Apartheid 1991. I could never figure out why she was always at reception. Sure, I saw other people behind the desk, but every time I needed something from reception, she was the person on duty! Did she sleep in the back room? Was she assigned to me? These questions, dear reader, remain unanswered to this day.

For my last request I decided to make it easy on both of us. No more assaults on her racist beliefs or jabs at her *Boerness*. I check out and ask her if she would "please phone for a colored taxi to take me to Jan Smuts Airport." She almost, and I do stress, almost smiled and said "they're much more dependable." The call was made and in no time, my baggage was tossed in the boot and I was crumpled up in the back of a late model, yet "much more dependable" Mercedes-Benz taxi. Upon learning that I was American, the driver asked the nature of my visit. I figured since this guy was colored I could give him the full story.

At my first mention of the ANC he cuts me off, "Ag, I'm worried that the blacks are going to fuck things up when they get in power man." Where the hell am I? Didn't I just leave the *Apartheid Hotel* behind? This guy hates blacks as well? I pull up short on my story. Now I'm listening to him bitch about black domination over whites and coloreds. I tell him about Mandela's speech the night before and how the ANC wants the colored community to play a major role in the changes to come. He says, "They'll have to really convince me why I shouldn't vote for the Nats." I wanted to scream, "You mean the same fucking Nats who invented apartheid you stupid shit?" I REALLY needed to get home.

At last we reached Jan Smuts Airport. I pay him his fare, tip him and then unload all of my spare change. I had the strangest sensation that the money was dirty and all I wanted to do was be rid of it. In the days before the terrorism of 9-11, you didn't have to arrive hours before your flight, and I found that I was working my way through customs with time to spare. Ah, customs; more blue clad apartheid apes to deal with before I could get the hell out of here. They instructed me to place all of my bags on the conveyer belt so they could be x-rayed. As my bags came through, one policeman/customs guard lifted my soft carry-on bag from the belt to inspect it. It contained all of my cassette interviews and Walkman.

He rummaged through it, dropped the tapes back inside and then flipped it back on to the moving belt. I didn't notice that the son of a bitch hadn't zipped it closed. I grabbed it by one handle, tipping it over, dropping practically all of its contents onto the cement floor. Cassettes, plastic cases, batteries and my Walkman scattered everywhere. He and another goon burst into laughter. As I struggled to collect my belongings and get out of the way of the other passengers, I blurted out "get me out of this fucking country!" I was surprised that my outburst resulted in absolutely no response; perhaps they had heard this sentiment before.

With heavy bags in tow, I made my way to the Sabena Airlines check-in counter. Once my bags were checked, all I had to do was "proceed to gate 12" and go home. It wasn't that easy. After so many sleepless nights, the weight of my exhaustion began to take its toll. Things seemed to be moving in slow motion, including me. It was increasingly difficult to think clearly, so finding "Gate 12" took much longer than I had expected. It was a mere fifteen minutes before boarding time when I finally arrived at the gate. I hurriedly presented my ticket for Flight SN 552; the attendant studied it for a moment before saying "There's going to be a slight delay in your flight. We'll inform you when we know more." What exactly does she mean by "'when we know more"? Christ, how much longer am I going to be here?

I was so tired, and just wanted to sleep…at home! Flashbacks from the Brussels Airport filled my head as I parked myself in one of the comfortless chairs of the Jan Smuts Airport. We all have our own ideas of how much time "a couple" or "a little bit" really is. So, what's "a slight delay"? After an hour of pondering this lofty question, my clouded process of deduction is broken by a rather monotone female voice over the PA system.

"Will passengers bound for Brussels aboard Sabena Airlines flight SN 522 please report to the ticket desk at Gate 12."

Since I was sitting, waiting and thinking at Gate 12, I had a short walk to the ticket desk. What could it possibly be this time, another delay? Shit, I might as well take up residency in apartheid land! Once at the ticket desk I discovered that the monotone PA system voice was attached to a very attractive brunette who informs me in a sexy, almost whispering voice that 'we're going to be delayed for at least another hour or more."

Then, after a suspenseful pause, she leans across the desk to get closer and drops the big news on me. "The details are sketchy, but we've been told that there is a military coup taking place in Zaire. (*The first stop in the flight to Brussels*) Things are not safe, so your flight is being diverted to Brazzaville in the Congo, just across the river from Kinshasa." Okay I thought, no big deal, we land at another airport, fuel up and go on our way.

Wait, there's more. "The flight will need to remain there until we can pick up Belgian refugees who are fleeing the violence." This can't be happening! Can my already rattled emotions take any more drama? Did Blondie plan THIS as well? Was this part of his "really get to know what's happening" itinerary? I reclaim my uncomfortable seat and resume my pattern of thinking and waiting and thinking some more. Nearly two hours later they announce that our flight to where ever the hell Brazzaville is, is now boarding. I was getting cranky. It seems that in South Africa "slight" meant three hours!

When you board a flight bound for a destination that is familiar to you, or at least a destination you are looking forward to visiting, you can pass the time contemplating a number of possibilities. The fun things you will you do when arrive. The interesting people you will meet. The exciting sites you will see. When you board a flight bound for "just across the river from Kinshasa" where the army is shooting up the place, looting and civil war may break out at any moment, your contemplations tend to lean toward questions like "What the hell am I doing here?" As well as "Am I going to die in a place I've never heard of?" From the looks on the faces of my fellow adventure bound passengers, I was not alone in these contemplations.

We had four hours to mull the exciting possibilities around in our heads. I asked the passenger on my right if they knew anything about Brazzaville or what was happening in Zaire. All they could tell me was "many Belgian nationals lived in Zaire", thus the need to rescue them from whatever shit was going down. They had no additional knowledge of Brazzaville, which only added to our shared anxiety. As we flew on toward whatever awaited us, I was struck by the fact that whatever was about to happen, had complete cleared my mind of what had happened back in South Africa. All of the emotional ups and downs, the images and voices that stayed with me night after night were now replaced by the imaginary images played out in my head. Before I knew it, the aircraft began a slow descent as the Captain announced the same.

Then, the flight attendant made what has to have been the most idiotic announcement ever uttered on any aircraft.

"While we are here in Brazzaville, all passengers must remain onboard the aircraft." Really?

Does that mean we can't get off and perhaps stroll along the river's edge just across from Kinshasa and watch the civil war? Had this woman suffered a brain injury since take off? As I considered the massive level of stupidity required to make such an announcement, Sabena flight SN 552 skidded to a full stop. At last I was…where?

This is Brazzaville Airport? From my seat, it literally looked as if a single blacktop runway was cut in the middle of the jungle. There were no other aircraft to be seen anywhere. Off to our left sat a small cement block building with a few windsocks gently fluttering in the breeze amidst a jumble of radio antenna. The moment we rolled to a full stop, a half dozen machine gun equipped military vehicles raced across the grass and the tarmac and quickly surrounded our aircraft. Were they here to protect us or attack us? For a brief instant it was hard to tell, but we all knew that this was some serious shit. As the aircraft engines shut down, you could hear a pin drop onboard. Passengers weren't talking to one another and flight attendants were not making stupid announcements; we were all too busy looking out of the windows as soldiers, armed to the teeth, began taking up positions around us.

Then, we waited and waited. Several passengers asked flight attendants if they had heard any news about the situation across the river. After an hour and a half, we learned that many members of the army of Zaire had mutinied. They were shooting up Kinshasa, looting homes and businesses and generally going on a rampage. None of the flight attendants knew exactly how many Belgian nationals were making their way to us; they did say there were only twelve open seats and we may have to double up.

As it happened one of the empty seats was just across the isle from me. For the next hour and a half, my time was spent thinking about all that had transpired during the past two weeks, about my wife, how badly I wanted to see her, and about the poor soul who would be sitting across from me, leaving everything behind. That poor soul was soon to be revealed to me. Just outside the window to my right, a large troop truck came speeding across the open field capturing everyone's attention. A truck of this size must be carrying quite a number of refugees I thought. It pulled up beside one of the machine gun equipped jeeps and stopped. Passengers from the left side of the aircraft hurried to the right side to see what was happening below.

A machine-gun toting solider rushed to the back of the truck to help passengers down. The twelve open seats were going to be more than an ample number, for there were only 5 adults; a gray haired man and woman in simple clothes, two other women, perhaps in their mid 40's, wearing khaki pants and lightweight jackets and finally, a young twenty-something mother, wearing only a short satin nightgown, in bare feet and carrying her infant child. All of them quickly made their way toward the aircraft.

With only five refugees, and knowing that there were twelve empty seats, I figured that the empty seat across from me would remain just that, empty. I was wrong. Down the aisle came a flight attendant followed by the nightgown-clad woman.

At any time other than this surreal moment, I would have described her as beautiful, sexy even, with long, dark hair and striking features. However, at this particular moment, this woman looked utterly terrified as she took her seat, cradling her baby against her breast. The flight attendant spoke to her in French as she wrapped both mother and child in a few blankets. Her low, calm voice seemed to ease the stress that was so evident. Within minutes after the refugees had taken their seats, the military vehicles sped away across the open field and out of sight. The aircraft engines were restarted and we raced down the runway and in to the air, as if we were fleeing for our lives. Once we had leveled off, the flight attendant returned to speak with the young mother. Still, clearly shaken by her ordeal, she spoke with great emotion, fighting back tears. The flight attendant noticed that those of us closest to her were all watching and wondering what story had just been told. What happened back in Kinshasa? She told us the young mother's story.

In the early hours of the morning, she and her husband were awakened by a phone call telling them that army troops were rioting, looting homes and businesses and shooting at random. They had no idea what was happening, but were told that the trouble was quickly moving in their direction. Feeling that there was little time to spare, her husband hurriedly put her and their infant in a vehicle and raced them to a safe haven.

There, they waited until transport across the river to The Congo could be secured. She didn't have time to dress or bring a single item. She was now worried sick about her husband. He said he would return to their home to protect it. That was all she knew. Now, all she could do was to wait until we arrived in Belgium and hope that she would hear from him. The fourteen-hour flight to Brussels was fatiguing beyond words. Factoring in the total six-hour delay, our flight time was nearly 20 hours. I could only imagine what this young woman was thinking and feeling all these hours.

The time was 2:30 a.m. when we finally touched down in Brussels. There were officials from either the airline or the government waiting to meet the refugees, it was hard to tell. I just remember lots of suits and ties and rapid-fire French. Those of us who were going on to other destinations were directed to a waiting bus that took us to a nearby hotel. As a result of our little side trip, Sabena was putting us up for what was left of the night, at no cost. It was nearly 3:00 a.m. as I checked in. Before our six hour delay, I had allowed myself to believe that I just might get a good night's sleep in Brussels; at least it seemed a remote possibility. Our original arrival time was 9:00 p.m., I figured on calling Charlottie, getting some dinner and then off to bed. What a complete fool I was for thinking that! When you factor in the past fortnight of almost no sleep, it made perfect sense that this night should be no different.

Once in my room, for the short time that it would actually be my room, I phoned my wife. I retraced the events of this memorable day, gave her the projected time of my arrival in New York and finally Philadelphia, told her how very much I loved her and collapsed fully dressed onto the bed, knowing that a peaceful night's sleep would be as elusive as ever. 8:00 a.m. and the guest phone in my room rang to announce my wake-up call. There really was no need. I had been up since six. I headed down to the hotel restaurant for my complimentary breakfast. Christ, this has to be better than my complimentary baguette and soft drink; my memorable first meal in continental Europe. That wonderful dining experience now seemed unreal to me, like something I had seen in a movie years ago. Thankfully, breakfast was hot, varied and plentiful. It was finally time to board the bus and head back to where all the craziness started, the Brussels International Airport. I was told that all of my checked baggage had been off-loaded from the Jo'burg flight and would be on my flight home. Since I had my most important material, the interviews, with me, I wasn't the least bit worried about lost baggage. As I entered the international departures terminal and found my gate, I was instantly transported back in time, well, back two weeks prior. There before me were those amazingly torturous plastic chairs, almost beckoning "come, sit, and be in pain once more." What the hell, I took a seat for old time's sake. Besides, I only had an hour and a half to kill, if things went accordingly, which they did. Somewhere around 12:30 p.m. Brussels time, I was in the air and heading home.

For the majority of this flight my thoughts were not of South Africa, Mandela, tortured comrades or nightgown clad refugees; they were fixed on my wife. I had so much to tell her, emotions that I wanted to share only with her. I especially wanted to hold her, because I knew doing so would ground me once again; something my battered emotions needed desperately. That, I knew, would have to wait until we arrived in Philadelphia where she would be waiting. Numb. That's the only word I can conjure up when it comes to describing how I felt stepping off Sabena Flight SN 225 in New York City. I knew there was a *"me"* somewhere inside this exhausted shell, but I'll be damned if I could feel it. All the adrenaline that kept pumping through my body during this journey, keeping me going day after day, night after night, had evaporated.

As I shuffled my way through customs, eyes glazed and clothes crumpled, I was surprised that I wasn't pulled out of line on suspicion of being drugged to the max. With bags cleared and passport stamped, I turned to head to my next departure gate and home. There, standing just outside of the customs area was Charlottie. I stood frozen in place at first, simply because this couldn't be her; she's supposed to be waiting in Philadelphia. For a moment it made me wonder where I actually was. Then she smiled, and just like some late-night love story movie, I dropped my bags and embraced her, holding on for dear life. You have to fully understand how deep of a love we have for each other to appreciate what this embrace meant to both of us. All you need to know is, at that particular time and place, it meant everything.

Witness History

Credibility. From the outset, Johnny Clegg stressed its importance above all else. Thanks to the support of Sipho, Blondie, Colin, Johnny and Barbara; and because of those I had met with damaged souls and those who were made stronger as a result of their pain; because of new contacts I had made on the ground in the townships and especially because of Nelson Mandela himself, *Amandla! Music of South Africa* and its host had earned unquestionable credibility.

As the turbulent years following my visit to South Africa unfolded before us, the program underwent a dramatic broadening of scope and an exceedingly more critical role for Sipho. This in turn brought about an expanded audience, with well over one hundred thousand weekly listeners. Sipho had the unenviable duty of reporting on countless acts of oppression, murder and the awkward baby-steps toward democracy. Many of these stories never made it to the network news, or were buried deep in the pages of newspapers; if covered at all. As of this writing, libraries and data bases around the world are filled with scholarly works detailing such events. I would be fooling myself if I believed that I could ever write anything that would capture their sheer magnitude. Allow me to list just a few of the many stories which Sipho brought to the Sunday morning breakfast tables of our listeners.

CODESA II, the Convention for a Democratic South Africa, which was supposed to put the finishing touches on *when* and *how* democratic elections would take place. One short month later, forty-six residents were slaughtered by Inkatha supporters in the township of Boipatong, bringing the talks to an end. Troops of the nominally independent homeland of Ciskei open fire on more than one-hundred thousand protesters killing twenty-eight. Inkatha and ANC rivalries in the KwaZulu-Natal region and in the townships around Johannesburg continued to claim lives daily. ANC National Executive member and struggle hero Chris Hani is assassinated. Five school children are killed by South African troops as they open fire on a home occupied by a member of the Pan Africanist Congress.

On and on it went. As the nation stumbled its way down a bloody path toward democratic elections, the guests on the program grew less and less musical. Regular contributors included Spokespersons Gil Marcus and Carl Neihaus from ANC headquarters in Johannesburg, and Godfrey Sithole in Philadelphia. Whenever asked, they were quick to join me to make the ANC's position on any number of issues quite clear, for both American and South African listeners.

At what seemed like the speed of light, this simple idea for a radio program had morphed into a highly respected resource for South African news, information and, yes, cultural entertainment. Despite the lofty goals and the highest affirmation of my credibility, I would still find myself taken aback by the issue of my skin color.

Perhaps I was naïve, but I was so deeply engrossed in carrying out the mission of the program, I had long since given up worrying about race, mine or anyone else's for that matter. Still, there it was, a white American hosting and producing a radio program about black South Africa! Remember, WDAS-FM was "the voice of the African-American community" and the majority of my listeners were African-American. I simply figured everyone who listened knew that I was white, knew that my heart was in the right place, and understood that my loyalty was clearly with the ANC and the people of South Africa. That, I believed, was that. Was I ever wrong!

At least several times a month I would receive a phone call that went something like this...

"James, great show! Thank you for this music and important information." These comments were always sincere. I never doubted that for a moment, and for good reason. As proud as I was of the program, I was saddened by the fact that there literally was nothing else like it in the entire country. People were genuinely thankful to hear music and real-time news from South Africa. In turn, when I responded, "I truly appreciate that." I too, meant it. There would then be a slight pause and perhaps a more inquisitive tone to their voice. "Um...James, can I asked you a question?" Here it comes. "Certainly, what would you like to ask?" As if I didn't already know. "Ah, are you a black man?" Here's where I would pause for just a second, as if I had to think about the color of my skin. "Nope, I'm white. Does that surprise you?"

Ninety-nine percent of the time surprise was an understatement. Shock is more appropriate. Many of my African-American listeners found it hard to believe that a white man would speak so freely about race. My very real, very vocal anger directed at the racist apartheid regime made it difficult for them to accept that a white person would speak this way. Once the initial shock subsided their response would usually be along these lines...

"The way you talk about things, I thought for sure you were a highly educated brother." These people were giving me more credit than I deserved!

"I could have sworn you were black." I liked this one because I could respond by saying "Thank you. I consider that a great compliment." That would always result in a laugh on the other end of the line. There were some who suspected all along that I was white, asking me outright as soon as I answered the phone,

"Are you white?" I would pause just for a second, building the drama, "As a matter of fact, I am." First, the shock; followed by composure, then, the next question.

"How did you get to be like this?" It would have taken far too long to explain the life experiences that brought me to this point, so I would just say, "that's a long story; let's just say this is the right thing to do and I'm honored to be playing a small role."

I truly loved these exchanges. The sense of connecting, of finding common ground was so remarkably powerful for both parties on the line.

Still, every so often a caller would be mildly adversarial, much the same way Liz was at Blondie's home in South Africa.

"Why is a *white man* doing a show on black Africa?" the caller would snap.

These were the types of calls I expected to be the norm, not the exception. I even mentioned this to Blondie while I was in South Africa. His advice,

"The next time a black man asks you that, ask him…why hasn't a black man thought of it?" Blondie's advice was sound, and I used his exact words. To my great pleasure, it would always defuse the conflict. In fact, it often resulted in stimulating discussion about race, preconceived notions and prejudice. Perhaps my favorite "you're white?" story involves one of the many prison inmates who were regular listeners. Sundiata was doing life in a Maximum Security prison in southern New Jersey.

One week I received a letter from him in which he related that on every Sunday morning at 11, he and several other "Afro-centric" inmates would listen in. Every few weeks I would receive a letter asking about certain artists or perhaps a question to ask Sipho. I welcomed any and all feedback. We began to correspond on a regular basis. We'd exchange our views and opinions on world politics and he even gave a detailed account of his trial in which he defended himself, and lost. One Saturday evening, an extensive TV feature about me aired on a prominent Philadelphia television program called "Visions". The program focuses on local stories relating to the African-American community.

As the program host introduced the segment about me, he said, "He speaks the language, has traveled to South Africa, and I bet you'll be surprised when you meet James Eoppolo." Surprised proved to be an understatement. The following week, I received a 10-page letter from Sundiata. It began the same way as the letters that preceded it.

"Brother James, I send greetings from those within my midst." Okay, so far, just another letter from Sundiata. Although, I was more than a bit puzzled as to why this letter was so bloody thick. It continued. "Those of us within were watching "Visions" Saturday night and saw the feature about you." That's cool. I was happy to know that the listeners got to see the program and learn more about me, and the radio show. The line that followed made me laugh out loud. "Holy shit! You're white!" Even after years of listening and corresponding, it seemed that the color of my skin never crossed their minds. He went on to articulate the feelings of some of my previously surprised listeners. The inmates just assumed that I was a highly educated black man who sounded white. As for the rest of the ten pages, he presented me with ten questions he wished me to answer. He provided his answers below each question. They ranged from explaining my non-racial attitudes and how they developed, to lofty philosophical inquiries. He closed by saying he would understand if I chose not to reply. Bullshit!

I spent the next week formulating my answers and sent back ten full pages. I waited anxiously for a reply. Would "those within" abandon me? Would they hate the white man for doing a show on the black man? My worries were for nothing. Sundiata's next letter was filled with praise for my honesty and integrity, and he promised continued support of what we were trying to accomplish. Many people would think that worrying about the continued support of *lifers* in a Maximum Security prison was somewhat odd. For me, it was welcome validation that I wasn't crazy for the years of effort spent trumpeting a culture and history that was far from being my own. There was a line in an article written about me in a South African magazine that I often found myself quoting to my color inquisitive listeners, it read, "It is clear that James Eoppolo was a black man in his previous life, which would explain his choice this time around." I continue to be most flattered by that description.

While the issue of credibility sometimes provided humorous moments, the reality was anything but humorous. Since the very first broadcast, Sipho "Jacobs" Ka-Khumalo provided what so many exiled South Africans living throughout the Philadelphia metropolitan area longed for, a well informed, sympathetic voice from home. Many had no reliable way to contact their families or friends back home; and as South Africa began to take one step forward and two steps back toward democracy, they tuned in religiously for the news and insight that Sipho provided.

It wasn't only exiles depending on, and growing found of Sipho, African-American and white listeners alike, were able to make a personal connection with Africa in ways they never imagined before. On occasion, the program featured very little music; instead we presented an opportunity for listeners to speak directly with Sipho. At the opening of these programs I would announce the call in phone number, and instantly phone lines would fill. My biggest worry doing a live phone-in program wasn't the risk of an obscenity going out over the air; it was whether or not my connection to Sipho would mysteriously vanish. Thanks to the paranoia of the apartheid regime, often times it did.

These special programs were a joy to host and produce. The level of excitement heard in the voices of those who got to speak with Sipho was contagious, especially when a fellow South Africa was the fortunate caller. Screams of joy, tears, words of praise; these were the emotional, spontaneous responses that greeted this distant voice from home. Calls ranged from heartfelt "thank you for all that you are doing" to specific questions about the violence in certain township areas, areas where family and friends were difficult to reach. Often the excited caller would speak Xhosa, Sotho, or Zulu thrilled at the chance to speak to Sipho in their native language. I'd have to interject a request for a translation; sometimes we got one, sometimes not. With each call it became clear that a much needed connection had been made.

If I had any regrets, it was that these programs always raced by, making it impossible to get to all of the callers. For quite some time, I had been telling Sipho that the listeners appreciated and respected him dearly. Bringing them together, if only through a phone call, was a distinct honor and privilege.

Another form of acceptance and affirmation came my way about eighteen months after my return from South Africa. When I sat in the office of ANC President Nelson Mandela in September of 1991 and expressed how the people of Philadelphia would love to welcome him to our city, I wondered if that day would ever come to be. Let's face it, seemingly everyone in every corner of planet earth wanted to meet, or at least see the man. I couldn't imagine the circumstances that would bring him to Philadelphia anytime in the foreseeable future. While my imagination may have failed me, reality did not. In the spring of 1993, it was announced that on July 4th President Bill Clinton would present Nelson Mandela with the Liberty Medal at Independence Hall in Philadelphia, the very spot where both the U.S. Declaration of Independence and the constitution were adopted. I'll let the official PR machine explain the significance of the medal itself.

Established in 1988 to commemorate the bicentennial of the U.S. Constitution, the Liberty Medal is awarded annually to men and women of courage and conviction who strive to secure the blessings of liberty to people around the globe.

Courage and conviction; two attributes which made Madiba an obvious choice for the Liberty Medal. But wait, our joy and excited anticipation were tempered by the addition of a co-winner; none other than F.W. de Klerk, the sitting President of an oppressive regime. To put it bluntly, this pissed people off big time. The local television, radio and newspaper media put a heavy emphasis on the story as prominent community leaders spoke angrily of organizing protests during de Klerk's visit. They strongly criticized the International Selection committee for not consulting with the African-American community about their choice of de Klerk.

Less than one week after the controversial selection of de Klerk, I invited Professor Martin Meyerson, the Chairman of the Selection Committee to join me on the program. He graciously agreed to the interview, his first on this hot button issue, knowing full well that I was among the vocal opposition. The obvious first question was "Why?" The Chairman explained, "The committee felt that if the majority and minority concerns in South Africa, two opposing forces, can sit down and negotiate a just settlement toward a democratic South Africa, as Mr. Mandela and Mr. de Klerk are doing, this certainly is deserving of the Liberty Medal." Knowing that he was on the radio station that dominated all others in the African-American community, he tried to appease critics by adding "a prominent Afro-American member of the committee voted for the selection of Mandela and de Klerk."

After his statement I said nothing, waiting to see if he had finished. He closed by saying "I know that you don't agree, but we stand by our selection." I said nothing. There was an awkward silence and he repeated, "Again, I know you disagree, but we feel strongly that we made the right choice." As I reviewed the recording of the interview for this book, I remembered how I smiled at his use of the term *Afro-American*, which had gone out of fashion twenty or more years earlier. I also remembered how I had to give the Professor great credit for venturing into the enemy camp so to speak. Before we even started, he knew that there was no way in hell I would ever agree with him, but he stood his ground admirably.

The anger over the joint awarding continued to ramp up as the weeks went by, but there remained a serious bit of work that needed to be done…the welcoming of Nelson Mandela. Needless to say, I readily accepted the honor when I was invited to join the *Welcoming Committee*. It turned out that I was the only member of the committee who had actually met, let alone spent any time with Mandela, thus, the invitation. The committee's first meeting took place one evening in a plush conference room located in a center city high-rise. Representatives from the Philadelphia clergy, local businesses, and various unions were all on-hand. A few members of the ANC and South African community were also present.

As we went around the room introducing ourselves, a communal sense of unity at being part of this historic undertaking filled the room. At least that's how the meeting started. It took almost no time at all for egos to steer the idea of unity right into the ditch. This was brought about by the first topic on the agenda…Mandela's first stop when he arrives in the city. Some representatives from the clergy, all from different churches, felt strongly that "it was only right that he be welcomed by the black clergy because the church was at the heart of the African-American community." Not so fast. Which church? Which pastor?

Those of us who were non-clergy members of the committee listened quietly while this battle was fought. Not to be excluded, the union reps cut in stressing that "since Mandela fought for the rights of the poor working man…a union hall should be his first stop." Back and forth, round and round it went. "Bring him here, bring him there, he must do this, he must do that." The Mandela Feeding Frenzy was in full swing. As voices grew louder and tempers flared, I snapped. "Excuse me!" No one heard. "Excuse me!" I shouted. "Listen to yourselves! You're talking about this man like he's an object." While I did manage to get their attention, I knew that I wouldn't have it for long. Still, I was determined to have MY say. "Even though he keeps a schedule that would kill most of us, he can't be at ten places at once. Show the man some respect."

That was about as much as I was able to get out. My little outburst did quiet things down somewhat, but the remainder of the meeting was nothing more than a rehashing of the earlier madness. At the conclusion of the evening I decided that I wanted nothing to do with the committee. To this day, I find it difficult to adequately explain the reason I removed myself from the committee. It has much to do with my total immersion, in my being so emotionally *involved*. I had come to know South Africans with countless tragic stories, saw the pain in their eyes, and heard it in their voices, like that of the elderly gentleman at Blondie's office, "Please tell the world what they are doing to us in South Africa". Add on the fact that having had the privilege of spending private time with Madiba, I got to see first-hand how he seemed to view himself, not as a messiah, but as *just another comrade* in the struggle, a struggle that was far from over. I simply couldn't get my head around what I saw as a well-meaning, but ego driven undertaking when there was so much left undone.

Let's jump ahead to the July 4th weekend. It was a blisteringly hot and humid weekend. Mandela arrived in Philadelphia mid-day Saturday, the third. It was a rapid fire meeting with the Mayor, city officials and the press; then off to the ultimate photo-op at the Liberty Bell, one of the country's most iconic symbols. Dinner with more officials and some serious fund raising topped off his first day in Philly. Sunday morning brought about a large breakfast event where everyone with a bit of clout managed to score a seat. I was on the air doing the radio program and recapping the previous day's events and highlighting what was to come. Through my contacts at Madiba's office, I had been briefed weeks ahead regarding his non-stop schedule. They apologized for the impossibility of having him on the program that day. Never in my wildest dreams did I expect to have yet another private meeting, so it came as no big surprise.

When my program finished up at noon, I was supposed to drive to Independence Hall in downtown Philadelphia to act as a sort of radio *analyst* during the Liberty Medal presentation. Oh, the best laid plans! Since President Clinton was the presenter, that meant security was massive. I wrapped up the program, hopped in my car and headed for downtown. I couldn't get within 10 blocks in all directions! Streets were blocked everywhere with virtually zero parking available. After an hour going up one street and down another, I gave up and headed for home. Added to the misery, I was beginning a summer cold and was feeling run down.

Hard to imagine, but this was one Madiba event I would have to miss. By the time I arrived home the presentation was underway. The sun was blazing as President Clinton praised both men saying "On this Fourth of July, look at these two men who are making history. Cynicism is a luxury the American people cannot afford". Of course that comment was directed at those of us who were opposed to the selection of de Klerk. He continued, "Here they stand together, a head of state and a former political prisoner, In their common endeavors, they are working together to liberate all South Africans." President Clinton went on to promise strong economic support from the U.S.

As the 2,000 invited guests and the thousands more who crammed their way along the mall listened, and perspired in the sweltering heat, Nelson Mandela spoke in the same slow, deliberate manner that was he style. "In the struggle for real change and a just peace, we will have to overcome the terrible heritage of the insult to human dignity, the inequalities, the conflicts and antagonisms that are the true expression of the apartheid system." No doubt the crowd was behind Madiba one hundred percent, but as the sun beat down relentlessly, I am certain some were wishing that he might hurry it up, just a bit. Of course his speech was greeted with thunderous applause and wild cheering. Clearly, Philadelphians loved this man.

If you want to know what de Klerk said, research it. Typical bullshit from the man, and I refuse to waste my time reflecting on it. Sorry, but as I said, this is not a history book. That night the cavernous Philadelphia Civic Center was packed to the rafters with thousands of joyful supporters, all there to see and hear Nelson Mandela. This event was a fund-raiser for the ANC sponsored by several of the most prominent African-American owned media outlets, including WDAS. Naturally, everyone wanted to have their moment with Madiba, so there was plenty of jockeying for a photo-op, and a place on stage. From the moment he stepped on stage, to long after he departed, Nelson Mandela owned the crowd, owned the city. Opposition to de Klerk aside, it was a tremendously successful weekend for Mandela, the ANC, and for Philadelphia. Everyone was happy. You'd think that peace and democracy had already swept through South Africa. In the weeks following the Liberty Medal ceremony the controversy surrounding the joint awarding quieted down.

In October, Mandela and de Klerk were jointly awarded the prestigious Nobel Peace Prize for "their work for the peaceful termination of the apartheid regime." All hell broke loose again. You can pretty much guess that the same fiery sentiments kindled by this award, had been shouted, heard, printed and reported a few short months earlier.

Unity

Long before Nelson Mandela's triumphant visit to Philadelphia, and the joyful unity it inspired, I learned an important fact; South Africans love to party, at least all of the South Africans that I knew. This was one of the seemingly inherent traits that drew me to them. Despite the suffering and oppression; music, song and the celebration of life are as important as the air we breathe. Early on in the history of the radio program my isiZulu teacher and friend Godfrey Sithole asked me to spin records and host a fundraiser for the Philadelphia chapter of the ANC. Everyone knew I had the best record collection this side of Jo'burg, and while bringing down apartheid was serious business, music, dancing and a damn good time was a much needed distraction.

The first party was such a success that everyone begged for others, I was only too happy to oblige. I hosted dance parties in clubs, hotels and in my home in the city. While I loved spinning great South Africa music that got people on the dance floor, it was the mix of people that made a lasting impression. All colors from all countries, all coming together to celebrate. It was especially gratifying for me when American friends and listeners thanked me for introducing them to my South African friends. For many Americans, both white and black, these were the first *real* Africans they had ever met.

There were many great parties, but a few stand out from the rest. In the summer of 1993, just shortly after Mandela's departure from Philadelphia, my friend Blondie Makhene and his wife Agnes came to the U.S. for their first visit. They were attended a record label convention in Los Angles. Blondie was hoping to increase his label's international distribution, something that never did transpire. After the L.A. trip, they were going to stop over and stay with us for a few days. I was thrilled. This would be my opportunity to throw one hell of a party for Blondie and Agnes, just as they had done for me in South Africa.

The invitations went out to the large South African community in and around Philadelphia, to friends and family, to listeners who had become friends and to our neighbors. We figured it would be better to invite the neighbors rather than piss them off with a noisy party going on until who knows when. We also factored in a number of *walk-ins*. These were the friends of friends of friends who would just show up, "We were told these are great parties!" What the hell! Come on in! At the time we lived in a long, semi-detached house in a very multi-cultural, very urban neighborhood. We cleared out furniture for dancing and by eight o'clock we were filling up. Of course our South African friends didn't show up until later. As my friend Fikile said with a hearty laugh, "You know South Africans, we come late, and never leave."

They brought booze, South African food and a desire to have a great evening. It gave me such pleasure to introduce Blondie and Agnes to everyone. They all knew his music from my program and were thrilled to meet him face to face. For Blondie's part, he was deeply touched to know that even with an ocean between them, his music brought strength and joy to this South African community. The booze flowed, the food was eaten and the house rocked as we danced to South Africa's hottest music. One of our neighbors brought his two teenage sons to the party specifically to meet Blondie and the other South Africans. They took to Blondie immediately, and he to them. Here were two young African-American teens meeting their first *real* African. The night was made memorable as we watched Blondie explain and then teach them the toyi-toyi. In turn they showed Blondie some of the latest U.S. dance steps. It was heartwarming to witness the special bond that was established that night; and deeply rewarding to have made it possible.

On the first of the two historic election days of April 1994, I phoned Sipho and recorded our conversation for broadcast on the next program. Sipho, like every other South African who voted, was beyond ecstatic. "Do you know where I voted?" he asked, barely able to control his excitement, "In Soweto, just a few blocks from Madiba's house!" I asked him to describe how he felt. In an almost giddy voice he exclaimed, "I feel like someone who has taken off something old and put on something brand new!"

We planned another "talk with Sipho" program for that Sunday; a perfect opportunity to let the listeners celebrate with him. It was wonderful to hear the exchange of joy and hope between people on this side of the world and their much-loved South African brother. This was perhaps the shortest one-hour program on record. The phone lines were flooded with South Africans and American who all wanted to celebrate with Sipho and one another. Naturally, historic elections in South Africa meant that it was time for an historic party in Philadelphia.

Freedom loving people all over the metropolitan area were primed for some kind of special celebration. I approached a large Philadelphia hotel and worked out a deal that would allow me to take over their nightclub for a *Freedom Party*. Then, I imposed myself on Kernie Anderson, the general manager of WDAS-FM asking that the station pay for food. "We can charge people to get in" he replied. "That would recoup the cost of food." I was having none of that. "This has to be FREE. You can't charge people who wish to celebrate their freedom."

By this time in our relationship, Kernie knew that when it came to anything to do with South Africa, I was relentless in my pursuit. He quickly gave in. Free to get in, free food. His only concern was the fact that a few popular sporting events were taking place that same weekend and I might be disappointed by the turnout.

I promoted the hell out of it on the air; then crossed my fingers and hoped for the best. My wife and I, along with several of our South African friends arrived at the club early. We set the mood with ANC flags, black, green and gold balloons and African print fabric. Then, we waited to see how many or how few would show up. The doors opened at 8 o'clock and people trickled in, I started to worry a bit, but remembered that South Africans always show up late. Where were the Americans I wondered? As in the past my worries were unfounded. By 9 o'clock the place was full to capacity.

This was the broadest mix of people yet. Young, elderly, white, black, Indian, Asian, people even brought their children, including one young couple who brought their five year old because 'We wanted him to see and be a part of history!"

The dance floor was packed during every song as this multi-cultural dream come true unfolded before me. At one point, I looked up to see General Manager Kernie Anderson heading my way. When he made it to the stage where I was spinning, he could hardly contain himself. Almost in tears he said "I have never seen anything like this in my life!" He surveyed the room and continued, "People brought their children here tonight. They brought their children!" I couldn't resist asking him "Do you still think we should have charged?" All he could do was smile.

When you witness a moment in time, and then live to see it pass in to history, the emotions one originally felt can sometimes seem trivial or naive. That may true, but I will never forget how I felt that night when I started playing "The Peace Song", the emotional plea for peace and unity written by pop-star composer and artist Sello "Chicco" Twala. Before me was a beautiful tapestry of multi-colored faces, and I watched with a lump in my throat as the people held hands and sang along. It was as if the South Africa everyone was hoping for was right there in that room. When it came time to end the evening no one wanted to leave, fearful that the magic spell of unity would be broken. We shot a lot of video that night and later sent copies to Sipho, Blondie and other friends in South Africa. Their reaction, and that of their friends who saw it, was touching. They were deeply moved by the fact that people tens of thousands of miles away cared so much, and wanted to celebrate freedom with them. That was easily one of the most special nights of my life…period.

Tall, thin, and only fifty-five years of age, Franklin Sonn, the *New* South Africa's new Ambassador to the United States was coming to Philadelphia for an ANC function. It was 1995, and once again I was asked to provide the entertainment. This was a huge affair, lots of big wigs, as well as plenty of dance party regulars attending.

What also made this an exciting function was the fact that the Ambassador was colored! Indeed, this was the new South Africa. After the dinner and speeches it was time for the music to kick in. I had concerns about how many of the proper, buttoned-down folks would actually get themselves out on the dance floor. I was no more than two or three songs into the evening when I pulled out one of Blondie's sure-fire toyi-toyi struggle songs. These always got the South Africans fired up, which in turn got the Americans going a bit crazy as well.

To my surprise, there in the middle of the crowd, leading them in the toyi-toyi, was Ambassador Sonn, smiling ear-to-ear and toyi-toying like a township comrade. The crowd loved this man. He spent the better part of the night on the dance floor. Yes indeed, South Africans love to party. The next morning he was a guest on my radio program and during a break, he inquired about my massive collection of South African music. I gave him a quick history on how the program evolved. The Ambassador then flattered me by asking if I would please make him several *mix* tapes to be used at embassy functions. With a smile he added, "The stuff we play now is boring as hell!"

Burn Out

Following the election of Nelson Mandela, the program's focus shifted once again. I continued to interview the country's top artists, some political figures, and of course feature lots of exciting new music, music that was now filled with praise for the new President and of hope for the new nation. Sipho's focus was directed less on violence and unrest, and more on the new struggle, President Mandela's efforts toward redevelopment and reconciliation. Reconciliation. The word stuck in the throats of many and prompted a recurring question that burned up the phone lines in the studio every time Sipho reported on it. Listeners who, through the program, had followed along the path toward democracy wanted to know, "How do you reconcile murders, assassinations, prison, torture and brutal oppression?" Sipho explained that the best answer the government could come up with was the Promotion of National Unity and Reconciliation Act of 1995. This would lead to the formation of the Truth and Reconciliation Commission (T & RC) the following year, chaired by the irreproachable Bishop Desmond Tutu. Its mandate,

To provide for the investigation and the establishment of as complete a picture as possible of the nature, causes and extent of gross violations of human rights committed during the period from 1 March 1960 to the cut-off date contemplated in the Constitution, within or outside the Republic, emanating from the conflicts of the past, and the fate or whereabouts of the victims of such violations; the granting of amnesty to persons who make full disclosure of all the relevant facts relating to acts associated with a political objective committed in the course of the conflicts of the past during the said period.

The *Rainbow Nation* had some heavy soul-searching to do. As cases before the T & RC were ruled upon, families of victims, and many victims themselves felt cheated beyond words. Perpetrators of outrageous acts of violence were granted amnesty for simply coming forward and admitting their crimes, often claiming that they were "following orders." When Sipho reported these cases, listeners were outraged. Many feeling that through reconciliation, the ANC, and even Mandela himself, had sold out the people who had suffered the most. If you want some truly heart wrenching reading, do an Internet search and read the transcripts, it's all there.

As the fall of 1996 approached, the stress of working my regular full time, extremely high pressure job, and the full time job of researching, writing, producing and hosting the weekly radio program was taking its toll on my health, both physical and mental. For months I never told anyone that I was close to burning out. For over 10 years, I had put aside all other interests and devoted all of my free time to turning an idea into a reality. The late nights, the many sleepless nights and the weeks without a day off came crashing down. When I finally told my wife how I was feeling, her advice was to do what I thought best for me, keep the program going or end it, it was my choice. That was my problem. The program was like my child; I created it, nurtured it and watched it grow in to something beyond anything I had ever imagined.

People had come to depend on what I was doing and on what Sipho was providing, how could I justify killing it? Nelson Mandela was President of the new South Africa; the program had exceeded all of my expectations, now it was time for a rest. For the sake of my health I had to end it.

I phoned Sipho one afternoon to tell him of my decision. He was shocked. While he clearly understood my near burn out condition, he asked me to try and clear my head and really think about my decision before I informed the radio station and the listeners. My mind was made up I told him. "This had been knocking around in my head for months and the next program will be my last." He was upset, but wanted me to do what I needed to do to save my health. Rather than tell the station management or the listeners that this would be the last program, I thought it best to do the show and then announce my decision to end it. As it happened, I was to broadcast the program *live* from a massive exhibition of African-America art at the Philadelphia Convention Center. I felt heavy and exhausted as I arrived at the convention center that Sunday morning. Somehow, I was able to keep the program on track, talk with listeners between songs and maintain the high standard I had always set for the program and for myself. When I finally closed out the program by playing *Nkosi Sikelel' iAfrika* just as I had always done, a wave of total depression swept over me. I couldn't get out of the building fast enough. My head hung down in despair as I made my way down a long corridor alone, I felt empty and defeated.

Out of nowhere appeared a very elderly African-American woman, tiny and thin. She approached me and with one hand raised to get my attention she stopped me and excitingly said "Excuse me, are you James?" I forced a smile and said, "Yes, I am." "James, I just want to thank you for helping me learn about my own people." Before I could speak she continued. "Because of you and your program I went to the library and got several books on Africa and I'm learning *our* story. I just wanted to thank you and say keep up the good work, God bless you." I thanked her for her kind words and we parted. "Keep up the good work." Her words and the look on her face were all I could see and hear as I headed for home. That day I learned that it was possible to feel both uplifted and depressed at the same time. There was no way in hell I could bring myself to end the program now, but how I would continue without collapsing was a question for which I had no answer. The next day I phoned Sipho and told him what had happened and that somehow, I was going to keep the program going. He assured me that things would work out.

For the next few months I wasn't so sure. The pressure from both jobs increased, and I was convinced that a nervous breakdown was right around the corner. Thankfully, much needed advice from a family member, who just happened to be a therapist, helped me to control the stress and bring about a significant improvement in the workplace.

This allowed me to relax a bit and to see the program and its importance with a slightly clearer head. Despite the lifting of the heavy fog, changes beyond my control were about to impact both Sipho and myself. Midway through 1997, Sipho's own struggle to find work as a journalist and entrepreneur made it increasingly difficult for him to make himself accessible. Several weeks would come and go without a report and the show suffered because of it. I think we both knew, but wouldn't say, that our job was done; there was nothing more to accomplish. Still, I couldn't be the one to kill this child of mine. Quite awkwardly, Sipho and I came to a silent parting of the ways.

The program began its 9th year, with no Sipho to file live reports. Fairly brain dead, I started to pre-record the entire show, not something I wanted to do, but since the program began, I had been working 6 days a week, sometimes 7, and I desperately needed a break. The world press had stopped writing about Mandela and the *Miracle Nation* and I knew in my heart that the program was weakening; there was nothing more to give. One morning in April 1998, I received a call from the radio station's Program Director, asking me to stop by for lunch. Lunch was nothing more than a smoke screen. I knew why he wanted to see me.

That afternoon I entered the Program Director's office and before he had time to look up I said, "So, you're killing the show." He looked up stunned and said "How the hell did you know?" Smiling I said, "Because I've known you for 9 years and you've never invited me to lunch." He started to offer what I know was a sincere apology and an explanation, but I cut him off and assured him that there were no hurt feelings. How could there be?

The station supported me from the start. I thanked him for that support, and most importantly, for doing what I could not do, end the program. The only regret that I expressed was the fact that now, the self-proclaimed "Voice of the African American community" provided no on-air support for anything to do with any part of Africa. Surprisingly, he agreed with me. I left his office with a bittersweet feeling. My child was dead, but I also had the weight of the world lifted right off of my shoulders.

Closure. Then again…

For more than 12 years, I had totally immersed myself in the music, politics, history, culture and people of South Africa. It was the right thing to do at the right time, and I have never regretted a single minute. Once the program ended, I finally found time to step back and examine the whirlwind that had swept me up. As if it were an out of body experience, I was able to analyze how intense those years had been. I quickly realized that I wasn't nearing a burnout; I was burned out, and more than a little screwed up as a result. Therapists call it PTSD, post-traumatic stress disorder. In fact, my wife's sister who IS a therapist told me that's exactly what I was experiencing.

For several years after the show, I couldn't listen to South African music, read the news about South Africa or study isiZulu. I even cut myself off from my dearest South African friends in the area. Emotionally, I simply could not process anything regarding my adopted homeland. My massive collection of music sat boxed up in my basement, bringing joy to no one. At one point I thought that my collection could be put to good use at Temple University in Philadelphia. I had lectured there on the role of culture in the mass democratic movement and was convinced that their African Studies Department would be thrilled to have such a collection. To my dismay, I learned that the entire department had been dissolved a few years earlier.

The University of Pennsylvania was my second choice. The head of their African Studies department was a white South African who had been a regular listener to the program. She told me that when she was first considering the position, she and her husband visited Philadelphia for a weekend. That Sunday, while driving around trying to decide her career path, she began to scan the radio dial and came upon "this guy talking about and playing South African music." She turned to her husband and said, "We're meant to come here!" When I described my music collection, I thought she would suffer a heart attack from excitement. She couldn't wait to meet me and review the music. All she needed to do was run it past the higher-ups.

I was content in my feeling that this was the right thing to do, until she got back to me with the answer from *the higher-ups*. "The collection would probably sit in the archives for years until someone could determine its importance, if there was any." Are these people idiots? "If there was any"? What kind of African Studies department wouldn't understand its importance? Screw the University of Pennsylvania. The collection remained in my basement, gathering even more dust.

Discovering that I now had an abundance of free time was frightening. All I knew or did over the last 12 years pertained to South Africa. There hadn't been any time for leisure reading, playing music, or long walks with my wife and our dogs. During that time I was fine with that, I had a job to do.

For my wife's part in all of this, she was the saint who supported my efforts from start to finish. She saw that I was burned to a crisp and was happy that I could now dedicate time to myself. Still, I was anxious about having nothing to fill the void. It took time, a long time, but I finally regained my equilibrium and was able to look back at what Sipho and I had accomplished with a deep sense of pride. With my once cloudy mind now clearer and content, I reached out to make contact with Sipho. This time no worry of poor phone connections, the age on the Internet was solidly established in the new South Africa. It was a joyful day when I tracked down Sipho's email address and sent off a message. Getting his warm reply meant the world to me, for it proved that even after the years of silence, we both recognized that we were indeed brothers. Distance and time couldn't change that.

I learned that during the years following his departure from the program, Sipho had converted to Islam and had taken the name Zaidi. He was also an award winning publisher/owner of the Kathorus Mail, a vital community newspaper serving the tens of thousands of residents in numerous townships around Johannesburg. It was no surprise to me that Sipho's instinctive brilliance as a reporter would once again serve the people of South Africa. Thanks to the wonder of the Internet we began corresponding on a regular basis, bringing each other up to date on our lives and the goings-on in the political arena, both in South Africa and the U.S. I was ecstatic to have him back in my life and to receive PDF copies of his paper.

In late 2005 Sipho wrote to me and mentioned that one evening he played a CD copy of one of our programs for his friend Sandile Memela, who was the Chief Director of Marketing and Public Relations for the Ministry of Arts and Culture. Sandile was so impressed with the program he suggested that Sipho make contact with two of his associates at the National Archives. Sandile felt that they would be keen to learn more about the program. My initial reaction was one of doubt. While both of us were proud of what we had done, I hardly believed that the National Archives would find the program of interest. With Sandile's assistance, Sipho was put in contact with Dennis Maake, the head of the National Archives. Dennis then arranged for Sipho to meet archivist, Melisia Shinners to present the history and share some examples of the program. She would then determine whether or not the National Archives would be interested in acquiring copies of the program.

Sipho already had several of the old programs on CD, and asked me to write a brief bio on myself, something that would help explain how things came to be. I obliged, sent it off and waited. Having had zero experience in such matters, I withheld any expectations regarding the outcome of the meeting. A few weeks later, Sipho sent an email to tell me that Melisia was thrilled with his presentation, and "yes", the National Archives most definitely wanted any and all the programs that I could provide. Both Melisia and Dennis felt that these programs were "of historic importance."

I had to re-read Sipho's email a few times to convince myself that I was reading it correctly. Sipho provided me with Melisia's contact info and instructed me to send her a rough idea of the number of programs I could offer, as well as a brief explanation of their content. After a few days digging amongst boxes filled with cassette tapes containing interviews and programs, I informed Melisia that I had approximately 65 to 70 hours of programs containing interviews with Mandela, other ANC leaders, dozens of South Africa's top musicians; as well as many of Sipho's more significant news reports detailing the turbulent years leading up to elections, along with the first few years of Mandela's presidency. Melisia wanted it all.

I set about the task of reviewing and cataloging the programs that I had saved. It quickly became clear to me that this was going to take quite a long time. In addition to detailing the content, I also had to convert each cassette tape to CD, requiring a real-time transfer from tape to a digital editor, then, cleaning up any blatant hiss or noises. For years these memories sat boxed up, out of sight and out of mind, serving no particular purpose. Now, they were evoking powerful emotions through the music, voices, tragedies and joys of the past. It was especially moving to hear conversations with those artists who had become dear to me, and had since passed away such as Sipho Gumede, Brenda Fassie and Marks Mankwane.

During this archiving process, I corresponded regularly with Melisia, updating her on my progress. A few months in to this undertaking, she informed me that she and Dennis Maake, the head of the National Archives, would be travelling to South America for a conference on film archiving and it was possible that they might have a brief stop over in Philadelphia. This was exciting news, we could meet, discuss my collection and I could provide a sampling of what I was preparing for them. A few weeks later Melisia confirmed that they would indeed be stopping over in Philadelphia. On the evening of their arrival I went to meet them for dinner at their hotel in downtown Philadelphia. Nervously I paced the hotel lobby waiting for them to come down, excited at the expectation of being with South Africans again.

Melisia was first to greet me. We embraced just as old friends would do. She told me in an earlier phone conversation that she was *colored* and lived in the township Mammelodi, just outside of Pretoria. I found it interesting that even in post-apartheid South Africa people still identified themselves by apartheid's racial classification. Turning back decades of racism was going to take some time. Dennis came down shortly afterwards and immediately embraced me saying, "I am so very happy to meet you my brother." Holy Christ he's black! For sometime I had convinced myself that he was probably some white guy left over from the old government. His name gave me no clue as to the color of his skin. Shit, now I'm classifying people by race. Fucking apartheid!

Over dinner we talked about the past and present, our personal histories and my collection. Melisia, who had been working at the National Archives for several years, explained that there were many "holes" in their history, especially when it came to people of color. She explained that the vast majority of films and audio archives dealt with white culture and white history. That was why they were so intrigued by my contribution. It was a joyous reawakening for me to hear the accents and see the faces of people from my adopted homeland. I asked them about their trip to South America and why their itinerary diverted them so far from their destination.

Dennis replied, "So we could meet you!"

I assumed he meant that they had chosen this short stopover rather then somewhere else, enabling us to meet, and I said as much. At that Dennis smiled and said "No James, Minister Jordan personally instructed us, to come here to meet you." It took a few seconds for his statement to sink in. "The Minister of Arts and Culture told you to come here to meet me?" Both Dennis and Melisia smiled at my disbelief.

"Yes!" he said. "He was informed about your collection, and wanted us to meet you and determine its significance."

All I could do was to shake my head, explaining how I never imagined that anyone, let alone the government of the new South Africa, would consider the program valuable, especially so many years after it had ended.

As it grew late, we made plans to meet the following morning to review programs and videos in my collection. My sister-in-law, who worked at a large law firm near their hotel had kindly arranged for us to use their conference room. The next morning I collected Dennis and Melisia and we walked to the office nearby. I brought along a list of the programs, details pertaining to each one, a few programs on CD and cassette, as well as video shot at our Election Victory Party. In the conference room I put on an interview that I had conducted with legendary guitarist and composer Ray Phiri while he was in Philadelphia with Paul Simon. Shortly after I started playing the interview, Dennis grabbed his cell phone and began dialing. I must have had a puzzled look on my face, which in turn prompted Melisia to smile and say, "He and Ray are old friends." I stopped the tape and Dennis put the phone on speaker just as Ray answered.

"Bra Ray, its Dennis" he said matter-of-factly. "Where are you bra?" Ray asked. "Right now I'm in Philadelphia with an old friend of yours." Dennis slid the phone over to me and I said "Ray, its James Eoppolo." I thought he'd blow the speaker on the phone as he shouted "JAMES E-OPP-OH-LOW! Where have you BEEN my brother?"

Ray was always near and dear to my heart and this surprise conversation had me grinning ear to ear. We brought each other up to date on our lives and careers and he made me promise to call him the minute I returned to South Africa.

Dennis explained the reason for his Philadelphia visit and Ray flattered me by saying it was "Well deserved and long overdue." After we ended our call to Ray, I played a few other clips and segments of programs. As they listened Melisia shook her head, and with a faint smile said "James, I am embarrassed to say that I do not speak any of our native languages. I grew up speaking Afrikaans and then English and can speak nothing else. You speak Zulu so well." I replied in my standard way "I speak it like a child!"

I then showed them the video from the Election Victory Party. They both grew quiet. Dennis was riveted to the video. Melisia became very emotional saying "I never imagined that people so far away would be so moved and so supportive of South Africa." It was yet another memorable South African moment added to a treasure of memories collected over 20 years. We concluded the review of the material; enjoyed a lavish lunch, courtesy of the law firm, followed by a quick motor tour of Philadelphia, mostly through local neighborhoods. I explained that while we didn't live under apartheid style laws, poverty, racism and the lack of economic opportunities helped to create clearly defined boundaries throughout the city. Some sections of the city looked very much like Johannesburg to them, racially and physically. As I dropped them at their hotel we embraced as we said our goodbyes and Melisia told me to phone her as soon as I finished cataloging the programs. I drove off with the African Jazz Pioneers blasting in my car stereo, feeling very proud of myself, and my distant brother Sipho.

With a renewed, energized sense of purpose, I worked tirelessly to complete this under-taking. As I was editing a program late one evening, I got to thinking about the hundreds of LPs, CDs and cassettes of South African music still gathering dust in my basement. I had pretty much given up the notion of donating the collection to a university; feeling that unless it was explained in detail and done in proper context, educators and their students would never grasp its importance. That's when I floated the idea of donating everything to the National Archives along with the radio program.

I emailed this suggestion to Melisia detailing just how extensive the collection had become over nearly 20 years. Once again, her response was one of sheer excitement as her large, bold type message brought a smile to my face.

"James, we will take it all, or whatever you'd like to donate!!!"

From start to finish, the process of reviewing, remastering and detailing the more than sixty-five hours of programs and packing up eight large boxes of CDs, LPs and cassettes took nearly five months. Nights, weekends, any free time I had was once again dedicated to South Africa. At long last, I was able to inform Melisia that this large chunk of my life was ready for shipping back home.

Melisia had arranged for everything to be collected at my home by an international courier, who would then clear customs and deliver it right to the door of the National Archives in Pretoria. Oh, if only things had gone that easily. Yes, the courier did come and collect all of the large boxes. I had filled out a brief listing of their contents which the courier assured me would be more than adequate to clear customs. Needless to say, I was completely taken by surprised when a few days later I received a phone call from Melisia's assistant in Pretoria asking me to phone the courier service, there was a problem. The problem was one of value.

Before the courier could ship the eight large boxes, U.S. customs wanted to know EXACTLY, and they stressed the word, EXACTLY what was in each box. There was more. They also required the EXACT value of the contents in each box. This was too funny, although I wasn't laughing. Eight boxes, packed full, now sitting in a depot somewhere in New York City and I'm supposed to know their EXACT contents and their EXACT value? Somehow, I convinced the courier that there was no way I could provide the EXACT contents of each box. As for the value, I pulled a numbers out of thin air totaling $3,500. What the hell did I care? The South African government was paying for shipping. I could have said a million dollars!

A day or so later, the courier phoned to say everything had cleared and the shipment was now on its way to Pretoria, arriving in a few days. I felt a great sense of relief, pride and finally *real* closure. All of these feelings would prove to be premature.Over the course of the next week I went back to my normal life and routines. My project was complete and the massive collection of music and programs was now sitting in the offices of the National Archives of South Africa…"how cool is that?" I thought. So, why hasn't Melisia emailed me to tell me that the boxes have arrived?

After more than a week of wondering I sent off a friendly email asking that very question. Her reply sent me in to what I could only call a rage. "We don't know where the shipment is James." Melisia wrote. "It was supposed to have arrived last week, but no-one seems to be able to locate it." Earlier in this book, journal, diary or whatever you would like to call this jumble of words, I wrote about my friend Colin "Jiggs" Smuts and his fondness for a certain four letter word. Suffice it to say, Colin's favorite word passed from my brain and onto my lips like a lightning strike upon reading Melisia's email. I must have re-read her message a hundred times, hoping that I was just stupid enough to misunderstand it. That wasn't the case. I could hear the words jumping off of the computer screen and in to my ears, "no-one seems to be able to locate it."

This did not call for a simple email reply on my part; this required a telephone call, an urgent one. In hindsight, I feel terrible for Melisia, she was so supportive and kind and we had developed a wonderful, long distance friendship. Now, she found herself trying to calm my fears and frustration from thousands of miles away. What she did know was that the courier service had delivered the shipment to South Africa. They had a signed customs receipt. That was a good thing. What she didn't know, or anyone else for that matter, was what happened to it. As a few days turned in to a few weeks, I was pretty well convinced that twenty years of my life, including the last intense five months were neatly arranged on someone's home stereo shelf; or had been sold off bit by bit.

One morning while checking emails, hoping that I would receive some news from Melisia, I saw that she had indeed sent a message and it was good new. Well, sort of good news. They had located all eight of the boxes! Where, you ask? Still sitting in customs, right where they were delivered. Why? This is the insane part of the story. It seemed that the South African government's very own Customs Department informed the South African government's very own National Archives that the accompanying paper work was insufficient to release the shipment. Just like their American counter-parts, South African customs wanted more information regarding the contents and its value. My déjà vu journey continued as I received an email from Melisia's assistant asking for more detailed information regarding the shipment.

My blood pressure escalated to dangerous levels as I fired off an angry email stating that I had done everything that was asked of me and if they wanted the collection, the collection that their own government was now withholding from them, they would have to figure this one out on their own. Silence of the email kind followed for the next few days. Not a single word came from South Africa. I felt guilty about my angry email, so I decided to just let things take whatever course they were destined to take, I made no attempt at contact. Then came word that the blockade, log-jam, red tape screw-up had been resolved and that all eight boxes were at long, long last sitting in the offices of the National Archives in Pretoria!

Melisia went on to tell me that the staff member who would be archiving everything was beside himself with excitement. He was in awe of how extensive a collection this turned out to be. He was discovering rare recordings that he had only heard about and believed that he would never get to hear. After a long, deep sigh of relief, I sent off my joyful reply celebrating what finally felt like an appropriate ending to one of the most significant chapters in my life.

In late 2009, nearly two years after delivery, the National Archives officially made my *collection* a permanent piece of South Africa's history. Sipho attended a brief ceremony and in my absence accepted a certificate of recognition from the Department of Arts and Culture.

Umuntu Ngamuntu Ngabantu

I have always been intrigued by the mystery and magic of how certain people enter your life, even briefly, and impact it in momentous ways. Sometimes, life shaping moments are subtle and their impact may go unnoticed. Nonetheless, they are every bit as substantial. In the case of my involvement with the people of South Africa, the impact they made on my life was about as subtle as thunder. The affect was nothing less than permanent. Many of those people were mentioned here, many were not, the countless artists, the activists, the numerous people on the streets of townships; heroes one and all. Each of them had a hand in shaping my life, in making me who I am today. In the earliest days of my connection to South Africa, my friend and tutor Godfrey Sithole taught me the Zulu proverb *Umuntu ngamuntu ngabantu*, meaning that *a person is a person through or because of other people,* those people who help to shape our lives and we theirs.

Considering my preexisting fascination with the topic, learning the proverb struck me as much more than a happy coincidence. For me, it has certainly held true. I have no idea when or even if I will ever return to South Africa, but that thought doesn't make me feel the least bit sad. Years ago, and especially now, thanks to the exercise of writing it all down, I carry a wonderful sense of contentment and peace of mind. I am at peace knowing that I remain part of South Africa, and that it will forever remain part of me.

Printed in Great Britain
by Amazon